CHARLES R. WALGREEN

FOUNDATION LECTURES

DEMOCRACY IN AMERICAN LIFE

THE UNIVERSITY OF CHICAGO PRESS · CHICAGO

THE BAKER & TAYLOR COMPANY, NEW YORK; THE CAMBRIDGE UNIVERSITY
PRESS, LONDON; THE MARUZEN-KABUSHIKI-KAISHA, TOKYO, OSAKA,
KYOTO, FUKUOKA, SENDAI; THE COMMERCIAL PRESS, LIMITED, SHANGHAI

DEMOCRACY IN AMERICAN LIFE

A HISTORICAL VIEW

By

AVERY CRAVEN

THE UNIVERSITY OF CHICAGO PRESS

CHICAGO · ILLINOIS

FOREWORD

✻

LECTURES given at the University of Chicago under the Charles R. Walgreen Foundation for the Study of American Institutions are designed to assist students toward an understanding of contemporary life in the United States—its background in history, its ideals, values, and institutions, its present needs and possible future. To foster an intelligent citizenship and patriotism, not narrowly nationalistic in their expression, and with thought and knowledge much more than emotion as their foundation, is a principal purpose of this Foundation.

During the university year 1940–41, "What Is Democracy?" "Democracy in American Life: a Historical View," "Democracy and National Unity," "Education in a Democracy," "The United States and Civilization," and "Basic Documents of Our Republic" were the several titles of the six series of lectures offered under the sponsorship of the Walgreen Foundation. As groups of addresses they were prepared for delivery to audiences of students. As separate volumes they, in similar manner, particularly invite laymen and not specialists to be their readers. In their published form they represent an effort of the Walgreen Foundation to extend its usefulness beyond the limits of the University of Chicago campus.

Without the gracious co-operation of the authors and the University of Chicago Press, this effort could not have been made. The road through the Press was much the smoother because of the kindly help given at all times by Miss Mary D. Alexander and Miss Mary Irwin.

WILLIAM T. HUTCHINSON

Executive Secretary, Charles R. Walgreen Foundation for the Study of American Institutions

PREFACE

✻

THESE lectures were prepared and delivered at the request of the Walgreen Foundation of the University of Chicago. They do not represent the author's spontaneous desire to write on the subject, but rather his willingness to co-operate with the University officials in their attempt to stimulate interest in democracy. They were prepared under pressure and without the opportunity to do any research in the field. They were delivered at intervals of one week, and each lecture was prepared during the week in which it was delivered. They are published just as delivered, without revision of any kind. They make no pretense whatsoever to new approaches or new materials. They are original only in the sense that they were written spontaneously out of the author's general knowledge of the field of American history and from the notes he has collected for classroom purposes. They were aimed at a mixed audience of students and

PREFACE

friends of the University of Chicago. They are published for the benefit of the general reader and not for the special scholar in the field.

AVERY CRAVEN

UNIVERSITY OF CHICAGO
March 1, 1941

TABLE OF CONTENTS

✻

xi

I

THOMAS JEFFERSON AND THE
DEMOCRATIC DOGMA

✻

AMERICANS have never been able to give a completely satisfactory definition of democracy. Theory and actual practice have contained so much more and so much less than any formal statement that something is always lacking for exact description. Some of our democracy is pure affirmation and faith; much of it is everyday practice and assumption. Both are essential parts of the whole. Yet they have often been in direct conflict. Practice has sometimes exceeded theory; social-economic-political conditions have often fallen far short of the ideals. Nowhere in the Western world has there been such "unholy contrast between the rich and the poor" as in this land of abundance. Nowhere have votes been so brazenly sold and public treasuries so openly plundered as in our American cities.

Nowhere have profits been offered as justification for such unsocial practices as in the American business world. Yet amid our slums, our crop-sharers, and our exploited miners, the name and virtues of Abraham Lincoln, as the great symbol of democracy, command universal and genuine respect from every class, and our profiteers and our political bosses are willing on occasion to endure actual sacrifices for the preservation of what they call the "American way of life."

These all-too-apparent contradictions emphasize the practical character of American democracy. It has been a faith which has helped a people to subdue a continent and to hurry American life along from frontier simplicity to urban-industrial complexity; it has in turn reflected and taken its own forms from the experiences, needs, and interests of this conquering people. American social-political theory, like economic and social patterns, was in the beginning borrowed from the Old World; that theory, in time, like the economic-social patterns, was altered by its own part in the remaking of the Indian's continent. Democracy was no American invention. The American way of life, which is democracy in action, is, on the other hand, a uniquely American thing, as strong and as weak as the American people themselves.

The first colonists on the American continent brought out little from the Old World which would, by modern standards, be called "democratic." Colonies and colonists of that day existed for the benefit of the mother-country—for the profit of those persons who invested in their founding or of the king who represented the nation in its expanding mood. The idea of local autonomy had no place in the scheme of things. English tradition, furthermore, dictated a stratified social order, and aristocratic government with privileges in lands, taxes, and office-holding permitted its establishment and continuation in the crude societies of New England and the South. Yet, in spite of undemocratic purposes and practices, appeal could be made when occasion required to liberal English precedents and liberal English theories which had already checked tyrannies at home. Furthermore, life in the wilderness was exacting, and the frontier spirit quickly asserted the right of the colonists to live comfortably and to profit by their toil. Free lands in some places and an expanding population everywhere nullified the force of English traditions and brought revolt against restraints and inequalities. Gradually new groups, especially in the back country, more democratic in outlook than those in older regions, arose to contend for larger privileges and the recognition of merit. An American order (in part, at least, the product of the wilderness and its ways) came into being—an order which had little respect for Old World traditions and which showed a restive temper toward privilege and custom. When the British statesmen moved to create a more closely knit organization of the Empire, and Parliament attempted to assert its control over matters vital to local autonomy, the American Revolution began. It had as its purpose not only the achievement of home rule but some readjustment in the rule at home as well.

To justify the positions taken in this struggle and to defend their own interests, the colonists dug deep into English political theory and practice. They called upon Coke, the Levelers, Locke, Harrington, and other more or less respectable individuals for support. Then with equal zeal they searched the continent of Eu-

rope for aid and took whatever Vattel, Rous-
seau, Montesquieu, and others had to offer.
With some original additions they found ample
justification for resistance to Parliament's taxes,
for the continuation of local freedom, and, in
the end, for their independence from the British
Empire.

In this struggle such basic American democratic documents as the Declaration and Re-
solves of the First Continental Congress, the
Virginia Bill of Rights, and the Declaration of
Independence came into being. The theory of
natural rights, of the social compact, of direct
representation, and of the application of the
common law were thoroughly Americanized.
In the first state constitutions and in the bills
of rights, the heritage of the peoples of Europe,
thousands of years in accumulating, was reduced to a formal American pattern. Even the
federal Constitution, reactionary as it was, emphasized the checks and balances of the English system and paid tribute to the notion of a
fundamental law behind all right action. One
writer has spoken of the Constitution as a return to London by way of Philadelphia.

It is thus perfectly clear that American democracy, in so far as early theory and formal statement are concerned, represented pretty much the rationalizing and speculating of several generations of European liberals, who had in turn appropriated whatever the past offered to them. It was native to America only in the applications made and the spirit in which they were made. It embodied the attempts of the colonial Americans to justify—with as good logic, law, and history as possible—the practices in which they had long indulged and the attitudes which they had long assumed. They accepted independence without wanting it, because it was necessary if they were to continue to live as they had been doing and as they liked to do. They would have preferred to have remained Englishmen if the cost had not been too great.

The point is that they had already, before 1776, created a native way of life, which contained much that was undemocratic, but which was in its larger characteristics strikingly in accord with the liberal thinking of the day. The American continent had taken a rather varied and somewhat nondescript group of Europeans, mixed them, and forced and permitted them to

live in ways—economic, political, and social—
which approximated the forms which liberals
had been advocating. Certainly American colonial society had not been planned or directed to
any great extent. It was a perfectly natural
growth, more or less accidental in detail. The
few cases where planning was tried were hope-
less failures. The emigrants were not selected for
any special gifts or qualities. They were not
above the general average of the countries from
which they came. The colonies got their share
of criminals and failures along with the mass of
common, middle-class people and a few aristocrats. The institutions which were set up were
borrowed and only slowly adjusted to the new
environment. They were not essentially different in form from those which the colonists had
known in the Old World. Democracy did not
characterize them to any unusual degree.

What America did to these people and their
institutions in the first century and a half is
hard to estimate. Unquestionably it greatly
simplified their lives, reducing society and all
it contributed and required, and magnified the
individual. Men were more important than institutions, and the individual relied on himself

and not on another for the things which sustained and enriched living. He did without things, and had what he was able to create for himself. The spirit of self-reliance grew apace, and confidence in man's ability to take care of himself matched the reduced services which he required to be done. All this, in turn, created a belief in individual rights—"natural rights." It encouraged individual freedom to act as necessity required. It led men to assume that they had a right to the possession of the lands necessary for a living; that they should have free access to natural resources of game and timber and minerals; that they had a natural right to form associations with their fellows for the better preservation of these rights, and to have a voice in governing and a chance to share in the offices which an organized society required. Added up, it spelled individualism and the notion that all things exist for the benefit of the individual.

Individualism, in turn, produced a sharp dislike for privilege. Men who stood on their own feet expected others to do the same; men who achieved by the force of their own abilities resented those who took what they did not deserve. The same temper placed emphasis on local government rather than on that which was farther removed. In a simple order men knew their needs and knew those who had the abilities to meet them. What could not be done by one's own self could best be done by one's own neighbors. Local needs required local wisdom.

Equally important as individualism was the American trait of believing in progress. Some have called it faith or optimism, but it was more than either. All Americans were on the make. They had come to the new continent to better themselves, to realize dreams, to find what they had failed to secure in the Old World. They had to believe in the future, and to believe that things would be better here than they had been elsewhere. They made simple starts. Often they engaged in the most elemental of economic efforts—hunting, trapping, fishing, or agriculture. They developed ever from the simple toward the complex. Out of a wilderness of savages they evolved towns, and trade, and industry. Little wonder if they should begin to think of America as a promised land where dreams were to come true and something more nearly perfect in government and society was to be developed than the earth had yet known. It was but a step from this to "manifest destiny"—God interested in America as the great experiment in democracy, the American Constitution in tune with the great moral law which underlies the universe.

Such attitudes as these revealed the new American temper as everyday living on the American continent was developing it. They typified the American spirit. They formed the national faith and took the place of a state religion. They represented the basic unity that lay beneath a surface mosaic of diverse sections and interests. They did not, however, show a completely democratic purpose or ideal. The individualism, which was so strongly developed, did indicate a firm interest in freedom, but a rugged individualism set free was most certainly already encouraging the rise of an aristocracy of wealth and the perversion of government for the purposes of privilege. Freedom could mean freedom to become unequal. Rugged individualism could exploit both men and resources and set up tyrants. Progress, in like fashion, was often confused with change of any kind and had already become an excuse for exploitation and injustice. It meant waste; it meant, too often, the substitution of individual material ends for those of social betterment. Even the Constitution might be used to defend tyranny under the guise of progress. The free individual, seeking his own ends and worshiping what he called progress, might be rapidly altering the face of a continent and piling up wealth and accomplishing huge material tasks, but this did not necessarily imply the use of just methods or the creation of a happy, well-ordered, democratic society.

Democracy was not something inherent in the transformation of a wilderness. American conditions might favor a democratic order, but they did not guarantee it, and they did encourage much that was undemocratic. Without the acceptance of moral responsibility and a positive purpose, democracy could be little more than the simplicity of frontier society. And while simplicity favored democracy, it did not assure it. In other words, democracy would not take care of itself while Americans gave undivided attention to the pursuit of wealth. It was not a gift of the gods to Americans. The main reason for its growth, in theory or in practice, lay in the existence of certain interests and groups which, because of weakness or losses of opportunities, made democracy a cry, a weapon with which to wage their fight for a change of circumstances. Democracy, like most things in this practical, material atmosphere, was of interest as it was of use. To live, it had to have spokesmen backed by practical interests.

Fortunately, the quarrel with the mother-country required the wide use of the democratic doctrine and emphasized the democratic character of so much in the simple American social-economic pattern. Otis, Dickinson, the Adamses, Jefferson, and a goodly company of able spokesmen thoroughly established the relationship between American interests and the democratic doctrine; they made democracy a weapon which future groups, disgruntled and neglected, might use. They made the tenets of democracy appear to be the basic framework of the whole American way of life. Ever afterward history, American history, was on the side of the unfortunate and the oppressed.

Independence won, the normal pursuit of self-interest was resumed. Reaction set in at once. Property and property rights quickly outweighed the individual who was not keeping up. The federal Constitution was a reactionary document from the point of view of the doctrines of the Revolution. Its bill of rights was a series of amendments added by dissatisfied elements after the instrument had been drawn up and submitted to the people. The rule of the few—of the well-born, the wealthy —soon began, and government lent its hand to the few who could invest in its financial paper and who gave their efforts to the building of cities and commerce and industry. The Hamiltonian theory and practice of government, admittedly undemocratic in character and purpose, but thoroughly American in every way, rose to dominance. The Constitution, by broad construction, favored this theory and practice. A new order of bourgeois acquisitiveness, heading toward urban-merchant capitalism, was in the saddle. Democracy, like the rest of the hindmost, was left for the devil.

Fortunately for the democratic doctrine, agriculture languished and fell behind. The farmers of the nation profited little from funding, banking, and tariff schemes. Markets closed by the Revolution were slow to open, and the burdens of taxation necessary for the new government fell heavily upon the farmers' shoulders. From New England to Georgia those who tilled the soil found little in the new order of things to make them contented and much to give them alarm. Leadership in the crisis fell for good reasons to the planter group in Virginia. To that state the nation had early turned for both military and civil leadership, and it was to continue to do so for more than two decades longer. The Virginia planter represented the highest advance made in American agriculture. He was the heir of the English squire, who had dominated the local life of the England from which most Americans had come. He was the champion of, and the proof of the soundness of, the physiocratic doctrine that the farmer is the only real producer and the rural order the best and soundest of all social forms. Jefferson was wont to declare that the ". . . . cultivators of the earth are the most valuable citizens. They are the most independent, the most virtuous." He called those "who labor on the earth . . . . the chosen people of God." John Taylor, his friend and chief supporter,

14

went so far as to declare that God had "pre-
scribed the agricultural virtues as the means
for . . . . admission . . . . into heaven," and
on the maintenance of republican institutions,
partial to farmers, depended "whether the
United States [should] establish a new era in
the world, or [should] follow the inglorious
track marked by the career of other nations."

What was even more significant, the agriculture of Virginia was in the depths of depression.
Tobacco, the great staple of Colonial days, had
long languished under British regulations, the
heavy burdens of indirect marketing, and the
wasteful practices of frontier farming methods.
Soils had been depleted as crop after crop had
been taken from the lands and as destructive
rainfall had carried surface materials off to the
sea. By the end of the Revolution a traveler
found Virginians "betraying strong symptoms
of poverty" and their houses "uniformly" of
"mean appearance."

A decade or so later another visitor described
the landowners of Virginia as generally "in
low circumstances, the inferior rank of them
wretched in the extreme"; agriculture in Virginia "had arrived at its lowest state of degra-

dation." The prices of land were down. Thousands turned their faces westward, abandoning both their fields and their houses. Even the more substantial planters were dividing their plantations into farms and shifting about in the search of new crops as their roofs sagged and petticoats were stuffed into broken window-panes.

Some said the soils were completely worn out and could no longer support a decent standard of living. Some grumbled because the middleman took more than his share of the returns. Some saw that markets were unsatisfactory. A few criticized the methods used in agriculture and pointed out the lack of crop rotation, of good plowing, of stock sufficient to give enough manure for hungry lands. All agreed that the policies of the new government, set up in the United States under the influence of Alexander Hamilton, had brought a new interest forward to contend with agriculture for control. In quick succession came the creation of a great national funded debt, the establishment of a national bank (with its accompanying extension of credit and the possibilities of enlarged issues of paper money), and protective tariffs for the encouragement of industry. "A monied aristocracy," "a privileged industrial aristocracy," were in the making. Government was being consolidated in the interests of itself and of those groups which profited by its action. Agriculture and local government were endangered. The Constitution was being twisted to serve new interests and to build new dominating powers.

To the defense of the farmer came Thomas Jefferson, Virginia planter and citizen of the world, armed with the democratic doctrines of Europe and of the American Revolution. He would go back to first principles; he would rescue the democratic dream which was the United States from destruction by greed.

In the story of democracy in American life, a new chapter of vital significance was about to be written. The democratic dogma had served its purpose well in the war against the mother-country. It had justified independence. But it had done little to alter the American social order as it had grown up from European beginnings. The influence of the crude wilderness had far outweighed it in determining American patterns. Hamilton's program and the ideas back of it had clearly shown that the course of developments in the future could be definitely back toward Europe and the past, and thoroughly undemocratic in flavor and purpose.

Jefferson and his farmers had to fight if democracy was to triumph. For the first time democracy became the weapon of an important element in American life for the purpose of giving shape to the political-economic structure. It became a practical force positively insisting on a greater equality and a more intelligent freedom. Thomas Jefferson began further to Americanize old doctrine—but, what is far more significant, he made it a vital force in everyday American affairs. His genius lay not in creation but in application. His great contribution was to gather from the whole body of the theory of his day the abstract principles best fitted to the actualities of American life and to make them have practical application to given situations.

From that day Jefferson's name has stood for all that is comprehended in a working social democracy. His personality and his spirit have gone marching down the years as vigorous and as potent and as inspiring as when he walked the face of the earth. Fifty years to the day after he had voted for the Declaration of Independence, old John Adams lay dying at Braintree. His mind wandered back to the friend and foe of his active years. He stirred, and speaking of Jefferson, muttered: "He still lives." In these words John Adams spoke for all time. Thomas Jefferson is still a living, driving force in the affairs of men. He stalks our streets. He challenges all who would seek privilege, or to interfere with the happiness of common men. He is loved and hated almost as much by living men as they love and hate their contemporaries. Theodore Roosevelt once wrote of Jefferson to Senator Lodge, with more than his usual emotion, "I hate that man." Others manifest an equally lively emotion in their love for him. James Truslow Adams, somewhat in terror, I think, calls one of his recent volumes *The Living Jefferson*.

I cannot take the time here to tell you of this queer, red-headed, freckled-faced aristocrat, who built with slave labor the finest house in all America on the top of a mountain, as much to be away from men as to get the view; this shy man, who crossed the street to avoid meeting others, and yet became the "demagogue" who roused the first American "rabble" to "revolution"; this farmer, who dabbled in science, music, art, and scientific agriculture; this closeted scholar, who served as governor of his state, foreign diplomat, secretary of state, and president of the United States, and yet wished that on his tombstone reference should be made only to the facts that he had written the Declaration of Independence, framed the bill for religious liberty in his native state, and founded the University of Virginia. I can only briefly outline the basic principles in the democratic tradition which he left for all those who in future days might work in defense of the democratic way of life.

Jefferson began with the fundamental assumption that the aim of all life is individual happiness. The purpose of the state is to secure and increase that happiness. All society, all art, all science, all philosophy, are to further the material and spiritual well-being of men. Men are ever more than institutions. The contribution to individual happiness is the measure of the institution. The instrument which does not meet the pragmatic test of furthering individual ethical ends must be altered or abolished.

Jefferson did not define happiness, but it is quite clear from some other statements that he viewed it as both an individual and a social matter. He believed, first, that man is so constituted that he always seeks pleasure, avoids pain, and can distinguish between them; and, second, that both morality and a sense of justice are inherent in man. Thus each individual knows and seeks his own highest good according to his own understanding, and tolerates the ways of others in doing the same thing. Happiness is found only in society. Enlightened self-interest causes that society to be characterized by virtue and fair play for all.

Back of Jefferson's whole approach, therefore, lay a deep faith in the wisdom and moral integrity of men, who, if free to seek their own happiness, would and could find it in society. His democracy was a faith and nothing but a faith. Commenting on this, Jefferson once said:

> You love them [the people] as infants whom you are afraid to trust without nurses; and I as adults whom I freely leave to self-government. . . . . I believe with you

that morality, compassion, generosity are innate elements of the human constitution; that justice is the fundamental law of society; that the majority, oppressing an individual, is guilty of a crime, abuses its strength, and by acting on the law of the strongest breaks up the foundations of society; that actions of the citizens in person, in affairs within their reach and competence, and in all others by representatives, chosen immediately, and removable by themselves, constitute the essence of a republic. . . . .

And Jefferson found the cause of most of the unhappiness of his day in the fact that men were nowhere free. Governments had become great organizations with purposes of their own —existing for their own ends and the ends of the few, not for the welfare of man as man. Their very complexity and scope of activity created a swarm of office-holders and dependents. By the favors they conferred, giving economic advantages to privileged groups, they increased their following and aided the few in plundering the many. They burdened men with taxes; got into wars which common men had to fight and pay for; attempted to do things which men could better do for themselves. They made men into subjects, instead of sovereigns. They governed men by force, not by "reason and truth."

The tyranny of the past, of the dead, was nearly as great as was that of government. Laws, traditions, customs, aristocracies of birth and of inherited wealth, cast their long shadows out of the past across the present and enslaved those who had taken no part in their creation and given no approval to their continuation. Dead hands shaped the ways of living men and laid their burdens on the backs of those who toiled.

Creeds and doctrines and church hierarchies were just as bad. The church, like the state, had purposes of its own, requiring service to itself rather than existing for the benefit of men. The great problem of the day was to make men free—to emphasize again the fact that the aim of life is individual happiness and that there can be no happiness without freedom. That was where Jefferson's program began. He would restore freedom to the individual.

The first problem was, therefore, one of restricting government—reducing its scope of activity, checking its power to create and favor interest groups, lightening taxes, etc. "I own I am not a friend to a very energetic government," he wrote. "It is always oppressive. It places the governors indeed more at their ease, at the expense of the people." Later, speaking of the difference between his ideas of government and those of Hamilton's Federalists, he said:

The doctrines of Europe were that men in numerous associations cannot be restrained within the limits of order and justice but by force, physical and moral, wielded over them by authorities independent of their will. Hence their organization of kings, hereditary nobles and priests. Still further to restrain the brute force of the people, they deem it necessary to keep them down by hard labor, poverty and ignorance, and to take from them, as from bees, so much of their earnings, as that unremitting labor shall be necessary to obtain a sufficient surplus barely to sustain a scanty and miserable life. And these earnings they apply to maintain their privileged orders in splendor and idleness, to fascinate the eyes of the people, and excite in them an humble adoration and submission, as to an order of superior beings.

He charged the Federalists with attempting to create a stronger central government than the Constitution had intended, to tighten "the cords of power" which the Convention had drawn "as tight as they could obtain them," and to weaken the state governments.

As to the purposes of his own party he said:

THOMAS JEFFERSON

We believe . . . . that man is a rational being, endowed by nature with rights, and with an innate sense of justice; and that he could be restrained from wrong, and protected in right, by moderate powers, confided to persons of their own choice, and held to their duties by dependence upon their will. We believe that the complicated organization of kings, nobles and priests were not the wisest nor best to effect the happiness of associated man: that wisdom and virtue were not hereditary: that the trappings of such a machinery consumed by their expense those earnings of industry they were meant to protect, and by the inequalities they produced, exposed liberty to sufferance. We believed that men enjoying in ease and security the full fruits of their own industry, enlisted by all their interests on the side of law and order, habituated to think for themselves, and to follow their reason as a guide, would be more easily and safely governed than with minds nourished in error and vitiated and debased, as in Europe, by ignorance, indigence and oppression. The cherishment of the people then was our principle, the fear and distrust of them that of the other party.

To check the Hamiltonian Federalists and to preserve the individual's freedom against the encroachments of government Jefferson had two remedies. The first was to keep the government close to the Constitution and the Constitution close to the intention of the framers and to its own phrases. He assumed that the government had been created for a democratic pur-

pose; that it was a government of definite powers delegated to it for the defense and increase
of the happiness of the individuals. He would
construe the instrument on which the government rested strictly and literally.

In the second place, he would preserve the
right of the people to alter that government,
peaceably if possible, by force if necessary.
Rights were more important than law and order. Speaking of Shays' Rebellion in Massachusetts, he insisted that it had given more
alarm than it should have done. "The tree of
liberty must be refreshed from time to time
with the blood of patriots and tyrants. It is its
natural manure," was his comment. On another occasion he admitted that the great
drawback to democracy was the "turbulence to
which it is subject." "But," he went on,
"weigh this against the oppressions of mon-
archy and it becomes nothing. Even this evil is
productive of good. It prevents the degeneracy
of government, and nourishes a general attention to the public affairs. I hold it that a little
rebellion now and then is a good thing and a
necessity in the political world as storms in the
physical. . . . . An observation of this truth

should render honest republican governors so mild in their punishment of rebellions as not to discourage them too much. It is a medicine necessary for the sound health of government."

What is to be remembered in this is not so much Jefferson's approval of rebellion as the fact that he was willing to accept such an evil for the better realization of individual freedom and happiness. No other thing in his thinking emphasizes so much the value he placed on the individual as against the value of government. Nothing else so clearly draws the distinction between the end and the means to the end. As a matter of fact, Jefferson did not consider rebellion as a necessity in democratic government but only as a respected weapon against abuse. "Educate and inform the mass of the people," he said. "Enable them to see that it is to their interest to preserve peace and order and they will preserve them. And it requires no very high degree of education to convince them of this. They are the only sure reliance for the preservation of our liberty."

The second problem in securing freedom for men was that of destroying the power of the past as it ruled the present. Men could not be free or accept the full responsibility in the social order until the force of other generations was removed. "I start out on this ground which I suppose to be self-evident," said Jefferson, "that the earth belongs to the living; that the dead have neither powers nor rights over it. . . . . What is true of every member of Society is true of them all collectively; since the rights of the whole can be no more than the sum of the rights of the individuals. . . . . The conclusion then is that neither the representatives of the nation nor the whole nation itself assembled, can validly engage debts beyond what they may pay in their own time, that is to say within thirty-four years of the date of engagement. . . . . On a similar ground it may be proved that no society can make a perpetual law. The earth belongs always to the living generation; they may manage it then, and what proceeds from it as they please during their usufruct. . . . . The Constitution and laws of their predecessors are extinguished then in their natural course, with those who gave them being. . . . . Every Constitution then, and every law, naturally expire at the end of thirty-four years. . . . ."

On the matter of debts and taxes he was even more specific. "Never borrow a dollar," he wrote, "without laying a tax in the same instant for paying the interest annually, and the principal within a given term and to consider the tax as pledged to the creditors on the public faith. . . . . We may consider each generation as a distinct nation, with a right by the will of its majority to bind themselves but none to bind the succeeding generation, more than the inhabitants of another country. . . . . At nineteen years from the day of a contract the majority of the contractors are dead and their contract with them. . . . . In seeking then for an ultimate term for the redemption of our debts, let us rally to this principle and provide for the payment within the term of nineteen years at the farthest."

And so with all customs and creeds and forms. There was nothing sacred about them. They were good only if they added to the happiness of the living. "Some men," said Jefferson, "ascribe to the men of the preceding age a wisdom more than human and suppose what they did to be beyond amendment." Not so. "We might as well require a man to wear the coat that fitted him when a boy as civilized society to remain ever under the regime of their ancestors. . . . .'' He would have agreed with the western man who once remarked that a fool can put on his own coat better than a wise man can put it on for him.

The Jeffersonian concept of democracy did not stop with a free man and his innate qualities. If man were set free to govern then he should be given every opportunity to be worthy of that freedom and to make out of it a happy social order. "Each person must be a man," he said, "be honest, truthful, temperate, grateful, and love man." Since the pursuit of agriculture best encouraged these qualities and put an edge on conscience that would not turn, Jefferson would provide the means by which "as few as possible [would] be without a little portion of land." "Those who labor in the earth are the chosen people of God, if He ever had a chosen people, whose breasts He has made His peculiar deposit for substantial and genuine virtue. Corruption of morals in the mass of cultivators is a phenomenon of which no age nor nation can furnish an example." Those who toiled in other lines were of necessity dependents. They were subservient, less virtuous, and "fit tools for the designs of ambition." The proportion of farmers in a nation to other classes measured the proportion of its soundness. We could rely on the virtue and unselfishness of our citizens "as long as agriculture was our main object." "When we get piled upon one another in large cities as in Europe," he said, "we shall become corrupt as in Europe and go to eating one another as they do there."

In the second place he would educate the individual to the extent of his capacity to profit by education. "No other sure foundation can be devised for the preservation of freedom and happiness," he wrote. "Preach, my dear sir, a crusade against ignorance, establish and improve the law for educating the common people." Through education a people could discover that "natural aristocracy" based on "virtue and talents" and perhaps find ways of placing it "into the offices of Government." He would buttress education with freedom of the press. "I am persuaded," he wrote, "that the good sense of the people will always be found to be the best army. They may be led astray for a moment, but will soon correct themselves. . . . . The basis of our governments being the opinion of the people, the very first object should be to keep that right—and were it left for me to decide whether we should have a government without newspapers or newspapers without a government I should not hesitate a moment to prefer the latter." "The only security for all is a free press," he was wont to say. "The force of public opinion cannot be resisted, when permitted freely to be expressed." "No government ought to be without censors; and where the press is free, no one ever will. . . . ." He was talking, of course, about an honest press which accepted its high responsibility to tell the truth regardless of advertisers and subscribers.

With all his emphasis on the freedom of the individual, Jefferson did not forget that man's happiness was to be secured in society. His freedom had ever to touch others. An equality between men had to go along with their freedom. Without government some men would use their freedom to trample on their fellows. An ideal situation would place all government within the man himself, but an ideal situation did not exist. So government was formed to restrain those who in the exercise of their own freedom interfered with the freedom of others, and for the purpose of adding to the opportunities for happiness which the individual could not supply himself and which the selfishness of others prevented the less fortunate from enjoying. Made directly responsible to men and quickly responsive to their wills, governments might render the social service of forwarding equality and security among men, which was just as essential for their happiness as was freedom.

Jefferson saw the conflict inherent in the situation. Freedom and equality were mortal enemies. If men were free, they might not remain equal in the pursuit of happiness; if they were kept equal by some outside force, they would not be free. Freedom was an individual thing; equality and security in that equality were social things. How could they be reconciled? Jefferson's answer goes to the very bottom, to the practical question of whether democracy can be made to work on any considerable scale or whether it is just an ideal based on a few glittering generalities. He merely said that men could be free and yet live happily in society, secure and equal, if they had the virtue and the sense of justice necessary and wanted a democracy enough to pay the price for it. It was entirely an ethical matter. A greedy people, bent on selfish gain, could not be free. Social justice was the result of good will and intention. If born of force, government must be a tyrant, forcing men against their wills, and democracy was at an end. The whole democratic scheme was possible if men justified the faith which Jefferson had in them. Democracy was something men voluntarily imposed on themselves. It implied restrictions, lots of them; but men restrained themselves voluntarily, considered the well-being of others because it was necessary for the good society which they wanted. Democracy was self-government within each man and not just a mere matter of voting and holding office.

There was, in fact, little virtue in political forms, republican or any other kind. Checks and balances helped to restrain the few, but unless the great masses practiced virtue and justice, because it was innate in them, the form of government mattered little. Men had to want a democracy and had to make it work by positive effort, if it worked at all. If the motives which characterized a people were those of self-gain, then the democratic forms would only magnify the inequalities, the injustices, and the corruption of the whole system. Here is the whole question of government activity and democracy. Jefferson thought that government was best which did little, but he assumed that men would for the love of democracy give social justice. If they did not and a good society did not appear, then government had to act and act as widely as necessary. There is no great difference between the democracy of Jefferson and that of Franklin D. Roosevelt on this point. The difference lies in the changing American people and the social order they have created.

It is not worth the while to follow the career of Thomas Jefferson as president of the United States after he had waged his campaign in 1800 and taken office while the Federalists stood back expecting the streets soon to run red with the blood of revolution. There is little value in pointing out the modifications which he was forced to make in his ideals when they had to be reduced to practice. If we catch the deep significance of the contribution he made to democracy we will understand that the spirit and the purpose were the important things and that variations in practice amount to little unless the great end he had in mind was shifted. And it was not, even though he was obliged to fight a war and lay new taxes; expand the powers of government to undreamed-of lengths in the purchasing of Louisiana; lay aside most of his dreams to meet the realities Napoleon thrust in his face; attempt in vain to check the powers of the federal courts, which were giving new application to the words of the Constitution; and only succeeded in checking the trade in slaves instead of destroying that great evil. These, after all, were but incidents in the evolution of national life, which proved that the great forces then shaping everyday living in America had to do with material things.

Jefferson's farmers kept on going down hill, until Napoleon, who was making the practice of democracy so hard for the great president, ironically enough opened profitable markets for the American farmer. Madison, to whom Jefferson left the presidency, was soon forced into war with England; war stimulated manufacturing and began to build the hated cities and to put the living of the many into the hands of a few industrial capitalists. Democracy was left behind, and the young nation turned about to face the great raw continent, abounding in new wests, which had to be conquered by coarse material ways and coarser material men bent on exploitation and the gains to be won.

But Jefferson kept his faith. As evening time drew on he sat each day on his hilltop and hopefully watched the walls of the University of Virginia, his university, slowly rising across the valley in the little town of Charlottesville. In youth and education there was hope. Democracy might yet become a reality.

II

THE WEST AND DEMOCRACY

✲

AMERICAN history is primarily a story of expansion. For over three hundred years our people have been pushing out from old centers, cutting into the wilderness, and transforming it into farms and cities and complex social-economic-political areas. Generally, but not always, they have moved westward with the setting sun in their faces. For this reason the term "the West" has come to signify the spirit and tone of one set of forces which have entered into the making of the American pattern. Yet when we talk about the frontier and the West, we are not talking necessarily of a place—we are talking of a process. We are talking of a set of influences under which one portion of the American people have lived their lives, and which has to a large degree shaped their thinking, their attitudes, and their values. We are trying to understand what effect this being so constantly in motion and so endlessly beginning over again has had on the American's mind and on his institutions.

Put it this way. In 1607 the American colonists consisted of a handful of Europeans on the eastern edge of the continent, with what they thought was an endless wilderness, filled with Indians, in front of them. These people had come to better themselves, to gain things, material and spiritual, which they could not hope to achieve in the Old World. Few of them dreamed of any drastic departure from the general forms of economic-social life they had known in their native lands. In 1907 a powerful nation stretched from the Atlantic to the Pacific; its people were consciously American to the marrow of their bones; its great cities counted their population by the millions; its factories produced for world-markets; its labor groups were bitter and complained of the evils of corporate capitalistic power; it had symphony orchestras and grand operas, art galleries and world's fairs; its farmers were sinking toward peasantry; slums and political bosses had appeared, and the natural resources of earth's richest continent were reduced to the point where the president of the United States was calling conservation congresses in the vain hope of salvaging the remnants. A process of expansion, of the conquest of the wilderness, of the erection of a complex, interdependent life, not greatly unlike that of other peoples who had known the Industrial Revolution, except in its extravagances and exaggerations! What was the effect of it all on the Europeans who began it? What effect did it have on the attitudes and practices of those who carried it on? For our own present purposes, what did the frontier and the West contribute to American democracy?

Many years ago Frederick Jackson Turner pointed out the significance of the frontier in American history. In his first great essay on that subject he said: "The most important effect of the frontier has been the promotion of democracy here and in Europe. . . . ." Twenty years later he wrote: "American democracy was born of no theorist's dream; it was not carried in the *Susan Constant* to Virginia nor in the *Mayflower* to Plymouth. It came out of the American forest, and it gained new strength each time it touched a new frontier. Not the

40

Constitution, but free land and an abundance of natural resources open to a fit people, made the democratic type of society in America for three centuries while it occupied its empire."

As has already been said in the preceding chapter, living on the raw American continent greatly simplified the social structure, gave wider freedom to men, and forced a greater self-reliance upon them. The wilderness was rather rude and blunt about its demands. It tore off Old World silks and buckles and dressed men in rude, fringed hunting shirts, with knives at their belts, coonskin caps on their heads, and moccasins on their feet. It forced men into log huts or sod houses and set them to doing the things which savage Indians had been doing. It altered their ways of thinking; lifted the family to new importance; gave the individual what he and his "pard" or his family could make for themselves out of the raw materials close at hand; and left them to live or die according to their ability to stand such primitive conditions. It made a hardy people out of those who survived, but it starved and scalped those who did not face the new facts and adjust themselves quickly to necessity. Someone has said that the timid never started West and the weak died on the way. A good woman wrote from Texas in the early days that it was a fine place for men, but hell on women and oxen.

In such a social order artificial accumulations fell away and men stood on their own crude merits. The questions put to the man or the institution were never: "How long have you existed?" "Who were your ancestors?" "What of your past?" "What is your social standing?" Or even: "How much education do you have?" They were, rather: "Can you do this rude job which is necessary to sustain yourself against the foes in the wilderness?" "Can you keep alive?" "Can you hold your own against this environment and begin to change it to a better one?" The measure was coarse, but it applied equally to all. Opportunity, furthermore, such as it was, played no favorites. The ignorant Irishman with his pick and shovel was as likely to find the pot of gold as was the Harvard graduate. The man with an uncertain past might be the man most essential to the present.

The early traveler in Illinois who reported that "a majority of the settlers have been discharged from penitentiaries and gaols or have been victims of misfortune or imprudence" was in fact emphasizing the frontier truth that a man's past counted for little; what had gone before could be forgotten if the individual could serve the needs of the present. Nor did the law, which the past had given, always secure obedience and respect. Vigilance committees took very short cuts to justice, and new western states, after borrowing constitutions from the east for immediate use, were soon indulging in innovations in legislation which paid scant attention to precedents. Bad men and lawlessness were as much a part of the frontier as the men who tamed them; both the desperado and the sheriff revealed a directness of action which was fresh and native. Andrew Jackson expressed the temper of a whole western world when he instructed a jury to "do what is *right* between these parties. That is what the law *means*." The tyranny of the dead was not heavy in the West.

Political affairs also showed the effects of these forces. The scarcity of men and the forced reliance of men on each other increased the respect for and the confidence in men as men. The social chain was never stronger than its weakest link. Ofttimes the lives of a whole group depended on the individual doing his duty and meeting his responsibility. He had to carry his share of the load and of the danger. He had to trust others, and he had to be worthy of the confidence of others. The marked dependence on leaders reflected this condition, pushing forward "the strong man," the local hero—the Boones, the Jacksons, the Bentons, or the Lincolns. They rose by the consent of those they led, and they retained their leadership as long as they kept the confidence of their followers. Thus men came to believe in the right to choose their own leaders and, to a degree, in their own ability to lead. If men could perform equally the tasks required in other lines, they could also perform those of government. Ralph Izard once wrote: "Our governments tend too much to Democracy. A handicraftman thinks an apprenticeship necessary to make him acquainted with his business. But our backcountrymen are of the opinion that a politician may be born such, as well as a poet." In fact, the greatest qualification for attracting votes was often a man's complete lack of any qualities superior to those of his fellows. To be "ordinary" was to be democratic; a man might be superior to his fellows but he must not feel himself to be superior. The following appeal for votes appeared in an Illinois newspaper:

To the Voters of Carbondale Township:

Having been strongly solicited by my friends, I hereby announce my candidacy for the office of Tax Assessor on the Independent ticket. I shall be opposed in this race by one of your best known citizens, Thomas Miller. Concerning him, I shall have nothing to say except that he is upright and honorable and he is my friend. As for myself, I am an Illinois Hill Billy, born and raised on a hill, two miles west of Carbondale. Outran the dogs on Sunday morning to keep from having my face washed, have gone sparking bare-footed and was almost grown before I learned the Republicans walked on their hind feet like people. Have farmed with a bull-tongue plow, worked at the Tie Plant, taught school twelve years, the last nine past here at Lincoln School and am a first class mechanic having worked right smart around a molasses mill. I want the office for summer employment and will promise if elected to make honest and impartial assessments. My school duties will keep me from getting around to call on all the voters, but I expect to spend the time I have between now and election, kissing babies, complimenting the ladies' cooking and bragging on the old man's crop. . . . .

Another political announcement, from the *Advocate Tribune*, of Indianola, Iowa, was even more pointed:

Having suffered a broken back in an accident at the Middle River coal mine, and being advised by my physician that I will never completely recover until I take a change for a time from hard physical labor, I am a candidate for the Office of Recorder of Warren County. If nominated at the primary next Monday and elected in November, I will not be a candidate for more than two terms. I expect by that time to be fully recovered from my injury and able to again jump back into active farm work.

Unquestionably there was much of freedom, both from government and from tradition, in the American West. The flavor was democratic even where the practice was not. There was also much of equality, even though it sometimes meant the dragging down of the higher to the level of the lower elements. But there was much else besides freedom and equality. Historians have sometimes forgotten that most frontier characteristics had their opposites, pulling in the other direction, and that undemocratic tendencies were also present. We talk much of the individualism which was so much a part of the democracy of the West. Yet we must also remember that the frontier required co-operation and was noted for its log-rollings, its house-raisings, its cornhuskings, and its other group undertakings. No part of the nation has been so intolerant of the man who did not conform to the group patterns and did not do things in the way everyone else did them. Its individualism was, as Carl Becker says, that of achievement, not of eccentricity; of conformity, not of revolt. The stern necessities of the first simple order demanded conformity in conduct so that each man might know what to expect of the other. That was the requirement for survival. The man who did not conform was a weak link in the chain, whose breaking endangered all. The result was a pounding of men into a common pattern, with a certain uniformity "in respect to ability, habit, and point of view." Deep-seated differences soon disappeared, and in the more advanced western worlds, public opinion condemned the individual who departed from the accepted or habitual ways of thinking or acting. Freedom disappeared, and the equality resulting was often as undemocratic as any other produced by force.

We have also talked much about the idealism

bred on the frontier. We have implied that those who went West to begin over again dreamed of building better than their fellows had done in the old sections. We have thought of them as men of faith, who saw things not as they were but as they were to be. However true this may have been, it was not the whole truth. The present, not the future, was as a matter of necessity always uppermost with the great majority. The tasks to be performed were immediate and material. There was little time or place for the dreamer among those who survived. The measures of success were in trees cut, acres plowed, game killed, and things accumulated. The size of things indicated their worth; the successful man was the one who got the most of things.

In like manner it could be shown that, with all his admiration of progress, the western man was basically conservative. A way of doing things once accepted became the right way to do them ever afterward. That with which he was familiar was the best; foreign things were dangerous. A smug provincialism characterized the West as it characterized the nation as a whole. Each man lived in the best region or town or state. Localities other than one's own were effete or backward. A dozen poems entitled "Where Does the West Begin" prove the fact. A few verses from one of them will suffice:

> Where does the West begin?
>   Out where the boosting's
> A little stronger,
>   Out where the hair grows
> A little longer.
>   That's where the West begins.
>
> Where does the East begin?
>   Where the streams are shaller
> And the hills are flat,
>   And a man is judged
> By his shirt and his hat.
>   That's where the East begins.
>
> Where does the West begin?
>   Where the talk is wild
> And runs to boast,
>   And to press your pants
> Is a crime, almost.
>   That's where the West begins.
>
> Where does the East begin?
>   Where the men use powder,
> And a wrist-watch ticks,
>   And everyone else
> But themselves is hicks.
>   That's where the East begins.

Where does the West begin?
  Where the laugh is loud
And the manner's rude,
  And to shave your neck
Marks a man a dude.
  That's where the West begins.

Where does the East begin?
  Where the women boss,
And the men-folk think
  That toast is a food
And tea is a drink.
  That's where the East begins.

What I would point out from this fact of conflict in frontier or western traits and attitudes
is that democracy was only half of the picture.
Freedom was often only a physical thing. It
was as often only a freedom to do things in the
way everybody else did them. It seldom ex-
tended to thinking. Freedom in action, worship of achievement, and measure in terms of
material things meant oppression and neglect
of the weak. If a man did not succeed in the
way success was viewed by the majority it was
his own fault, and he was not to be pitied. An
aristocracy of achievement came to mean an
aristocracy of wealth—the very worst kind of
aristocracy. If the past lost its power to op-

press men, the present gained in that power. Habit and provincialism both restrained; government by majorities tyrannized over its own minorities; equality was an abstraction quickly forgotten where success consisted of becoming unequal in the possession of material things, which gave all power by popular consent.

When we recognize these facts we are in a position to understand that much which has passed for democracy in the United States does not qualify on closer examination. It has been little more than the simplicity and opportunity which a raw continent has produced. Seldom has it been the choice of men or a matter of their own creation. The United States has been fortunate in having a frontier throughout most of its history and a West for all of it. Both have had strong democratic forces at work in them, which have leavened the whole and made freedom and equality realities in the face of other forces which have pulled against them.

These forces, however, have not constituted the West's greatest contribution to the democratic way. The positive, intentional drive for democracy has been born of something other than the drift of affairs. One thing has characterized all of our wests and all of our frontiers. They have been thwarted and bitter. They have been regions of protest. They have been conscious of their own merits, sensitive to their rights, and resentful of neglect. They have constituted a more or less permanent region and interest which have wielded the democratic ideal as a weapon. Out of the American West have come the men and the movements which, after the days of Thomas Jefferson, have kept strong the democratic faith. Far more important than their simple practice of American democracy have been their protests and their revolts. From Andrew Jackson to Abraham Lincoln and William Jennings Bryan they have fought their own fights, but they have kept the democratic dogma alive in doing so.

Men who went to our early wests met more or less primitive conditions. They had to sacrifice comforts and safety; they had to endure hardships as a rule. But they expected ultimately to better themselves and to profit by exploiting the natural resources of the new regions and by the unearned increments, social and economic. They had no intention whatsoever of remaining in an inferior condition. They were not unselfish, and they were in a great hurry to get ahead. They generally found, however, that their dreams surpassed realities. Progress was slow. Nature was stubborn. They had to endure what seemed to be more than their share of hard times.

In all cases western welfare and progress depended, first, on an easy access to lands and the riches which they might contain; second, on easy financial arrangements and institutions through which they could pay for lands and gather nature's riches; third, on satisfactory ways to markets—which generally meant internal improvements in the form of work on rivers, canals, roads, railroads, etc.; and, fourth, on profitable markets in which they could sell their surplus. Most of these things the individual, or even the whole western region, could not secure for himself or itself. The wests were dependent on the wealth of the older regions or on the national government for them. The whole matter of progress was in the hands of others to a large degree. That meant trouble for the impatient pioneer. The eastern capitalist wanted both security for his loans and investments and goodly profits on them. He was

in a speculative mood. He was not much inclined to value the great work of pushing back
the wilderness in which the pioneer was engaged. He was of a mind to take his pound of
flesh and to view with alarm the extravagant
speed with which the West was doing things.

Government, in the hands of the older sections, was equally conservative. Legislation
for the granting of free lands to actual settlers,
large appropriations for the digging of canals,
the clearing of rivers and harbors, the improvement of highways, and for the encouragement
of home markets came slowly if at all. Government of the people seemed to be government in
behalf of those who had remained by the family
firesides and not for those who had risked their
scalps in crowding the Indians. The republican system of government was playing favorites. Democracy was losing ground. Something ought to be done about it. From Jefferson
to Bryan these were the western attitudes. Re-
sentment and revolt, mixed in with stretches of
unjustifiable optimism, characterized their temper. In that temper lay the hope of democracy.

In the decade following Thomas Jefferson's
failure to rescue the American farmer with the

democratic appeal, the embargo and the War of 1812 at last cut the lingering colonial ties which still bound us to Europe and turned the nation about to face westward. Up to this time the United States had looked toward the Atlantic. Its commerce had been foreign commerce, its great problems those of a neutral in European struggles, its prominent leaders had been diplomats, even its political parties had formed in part over European issues. In the northeastern corner of the nation merchant capitalism and soon industrial capitalism developed. In the South a new and greater staple, cotton, gave new strength to the plantation system and new life to Negro slavery. More important than either, a great new West opened across the mountains. We became, as John Randolph said, a great land animal dragging its bulky form toward the Pacific. Our problems and interests were American—lands, internal improvements, markets, finances. National leaders came out of the West to dominate and direct the nation's course—the young Henry Clay, the patriotic John C. Calhoun, the aggressive Thomas H. Benton, the forceful Andrew Jackson. People poured west at such a rate that the traveler spoke of the whole nation breaking up and betaking itself to the other side of the Allegheny Mountains. The Monroe Doctrine announced to the world that we were completely occupied with our own problems, had possessed ourselves of the continent, and could not tolerate other systems extending farther in this hemisphere. The American period of American history was opening. In 1828 it signaled its complete arrival in the election of Andrew Jackson to the presidency of the United States.

Jackson's election has been hailed by most historians as the triumph of democracy over aristocracy. The most recent college textbook that I have been able to find says:

> A new conception of democracy was abroad in the land. No longer were the people satisfied, as Jefferson had supposed they would be, to fill offices from among their betters. Popular rule had come to mean that the common people should choose their rulers from among themselves, and by 1828 the extension of the suffrage had gone to such lengths that an aristocratic Adams in a contest with a democratic Jackson had not the remotest chance to win.

This same text speaks of "this march of democracy" and tells how "one after another the citadels of aristocracy fell before the attack," until at last democracy was triumphant in Jackson.

With the emphasis on the part which western states had played in liberalizing the franchise and the wider participation of common men in political affairs, I have no quarrel. But I would like to suggest that the forces which brought Jackson to the presidency had much more to do with western resentments than with any western belief in abstract democracy. The West had some specific grievances. Interests, not ideals, were at stake. Jackson was a self-made man and a popular hero, but he had risen well above the common levels of Tennessee society long before he reached the White House. The Hermitage, with its great white pillars and its wide, open hallway, was one of the most splendid mansions in the whole country. Jackson's slaves were numerous; his connections with local bankers and land speculators were intimate. The ladies found his manners excellent, and those who came in close contact with him found his intelligence high. He was certainly no "wool-hat boy" in 1828. The appeal he made to the men of his section and of other sections was not that of a demagogue.

What was more important than Jackson's raw democracy was the fact that he had been cheated, or was thought to have been cheated, out of the presidency in 1825 by a "corrupt bargain" between John Quincy Adams and Henry Clay; that he came from the newer West and represented its interests; that the West, the agricultural South, the rural parts of New England and the Middle States, and the lesser folk in the old shipping centers were all in revolt against those who had been in power because of their failure to give prosperity and the kind of legislation which they wished.

The attitudes shown at Jackson's inaugural were those of class consciousness. Great crowds in homespun gathered in Washington and over-ran the public buildings. They tramped through the White House (their White House) with their muddy boots, stood on the damask-covered chairs, and nearly squeezed their president to death in the effort to drink his punch and to shake his hand. Then they went after the public offices in the same manner—a wild scramble for the spoils. The idea was that the East ("the aristocrats"), which had so long neglected the interests of the West ("the com-

mon people"), had now surrendered the citadel
and occupation had begun. The whole pro-
cedure was thoroughly western and in keeping
with western ideas of government and its uses.
But it was not, as some historians would have
us believe, one of those revolutions in the interest of freedom which Thomas Jefferson had talked about. It was related to his thinking only in
so far as government was taking an awful beat-
ing. It was merely a change of rulers. Government was not diminished; in fact, it soon increased its powers along certain lines. Men were
soon talking about the "reign" of Andrew
Jackson.

What did it all mean in terms of democracy in
American life? Unquestionably, more men had
voted for Andrew Jackson than for any of his
predecessors. But does the size of a candidate's
vote measure the quality and quantity of his
democracy and that of the forces behind him?
Had Jackson come forward with some clear-cut
program for the increase of the happiness of
common men? Did his election mean that there
were to be social-economic changes in the interest of greater freedom and equality? There
can be but one answer, and that is "No!" Jack-

son had no great democratic course blocked out. His position on most of the important issues of the day was not clear even to his closest friends. Honest scholars doubt whether he himself knew what he thought about these issues or what he intended to do with his administration. Seemingly he was totally unconscious of the evils of the factory system or of Negro slavery which had come to plague the nation and to force upon democracy its most serious problems. The truth was that Jackson was only the symbol of the rise of a new West in American life and the ability of common men to put a leader of their own choosing in the presidential chair. His followers undoubtedly expected him to tumble down a few aristocrats; he himself probably had ideas of the same kind. But what lay ahead in American life for democracy depended entirely, as it had depended in Jefferson's day, on the necessity for an appeal to its doctrines as a way of securing rights and interests on the part of the disgruntled and revolting elements. In this case the West and the poor had revolted and named a president. Their happiness and well-being depended not on being let alone and freed from tradition but on being able quickly to get hold of the great natural resources of the continent and rapidly to develop mature societies. Democracy meant the having of material things in new degree, the assistance of government in acquiring these things. In concrete terms it meant keeping control of the government and its offices through the perfection of the party machine; the passage of legislation which would make the public lands easily available to settlers; the destruction of the national bank, which had interfered with the most rapid western advances by its sound policies; the development of better markets by tariff legislation; and the improvement of ways to those markets. Equality and privilege were both potentially present in such a program.

What I am trying to emphasize is that democracy "had become bread." It meant very concrete things to be gained through political control. The politician would keep his place and the party its success through services rendered, and services rendered or not rendered would indicate whether democracy was functioning properly or not. Around group and sectional interests party conflicts would rage.

Parties, in turn, would reflect sectional and group interests. Democracy would become a cry to promote party ends. The great natural resources of the continent might be used for the common good under the legislation passed by those in power or they might be used to insure party success and the advancement of those who would exploit both the natural resources and the common people. Party government might become interest government and campaigns emotional debaucheries to get votes. Revolt would be harder now. Reform would have to be political reform before it could become social-economic reform in the interests of human happiness. The third party—always the party of revolt—would become the guardian of the democratic dogma.

What the role of the democratic dogma was to be in such a tangle was quickly revealed in Jackson's war against the bank and in the land and tariff struggles. In each case the cause of a section or of an interest became the cause of democracy. The national bank had won the enmity of western men by the restraints it placed on the "wildcat" practices of their state banks and by its strict foreclosures on western properties. Some of its officials had dabbled in politics and some of its financial practices might be open to question, yet no one could doubt the benefits it had bestowed. The issue of one kind of a financial institution as against another was merely a matter of opinion. Jackson, however, dealt with the bank as western men would have had him do and based his attack squarely on democratic principles. He called it "the monster," a "hydra of corruption, dangerous to our liberties everywhere." His veto message of the bill rechartering the bank spoke of "the artificial distinctions" produced by law to "make the rich richer and the potent more powerful," and declared that the "humble members of society, the farmer, mechanics, the laborers, who have neither the time nor the means of securing like favors to themselves" had a right to complain. Later he charged that "a monied aristocracy of the few" was waging a war "against the Democracy of numbers; the prosperous to make the honest labourers hewers of wood & drawers of water to the monied aristocracy of the country thro the credit and paper system." He was defending his West with perfectly good Jeffersonian assertions. He was acting, however, considerably like a dictator.

In the struggle for easier access to public lands, western men again raised the cry of democracy. Possession of land was a natural right. As a western congressman said:

... Every human being has, by the stern law of nature, an inalienable right to a reasonable share and proportionate part of it, upon which to obtain a subsistence: as much so as he has to inflate his lungs with the air that he breathes, and by which he is surrounded, or to drink of the water with which our country is so abundantly blessed—a right and a privilege which, innate in itself, was [sic] derived from the Supreme Being.

One state assembly, in favoring legislation for the actual settler, declared:

Our country is peculiarly the asylum of the oppressed and emphatically the poor man's home. Every law, then, which opens to the poor man the way to independence, which lifts him above the grade of the tenant, which gives to him and his children a permanent and abiding resting place on the soil, not only subserves the cause of Humanity but advances and maintains the fundamental principles of our Government.

Men who stole public lands were not "violators of the law." They were, said an Alabama senator in 1830, "meritorious individuals, because they have been the pioneers to all the new settlements in the West and South-west." "The enhanced value given to the land" which these men improved gave added value to all other lands and in the end thus benefited the public treasury. The laws which punished the squatter, said Sibley of Minnesota, were a "disgrace to the country and to the nineteenth century. . . . ." Democracy required a liberal hand with the public domain. To use it for revenue, to permit eastern capitalists to speculate on it, were un-American. "God intended, ... as good governments and good men desired," as Caruthers of Missouri said, "that they should go into the hands of the people, for occupation, for cultivation, for ownership."

To balance the picture we need only to notice that Henry Clay's tariff schemes were justified on the same lofty democratic ground. American economic life was too simple for the highest development of the individual and his happiness. English rivalry in manufactures kept him in a backward state. The farmer's son had to become a farmer; the towns offered only simple mercantile pursuits or the chance to go to sea. To be truly free, to have the complete opportunity for equality, America must diversify her economic life by protective tariffs. In a simple society the law of diminishing returns and the iron law of wages doomed mankind to a losing fight. Men like Henry Carey would put to rout the cold determinism of Malthus and Ricardo, and by national planning behind protective tariff walls achieve a well-balanced, self-sufficing social order in which plenty and justice would dominate.

Here was a new kind of democracy, a new use for the democratic dogma. The West had risen to national control and had brought with it to power new conceptions of individual freedom and happiness, new uses to which government might be put, new agencies for control within the forms of government. The party machine, the nominating convention, and the spoils system had come to completion. The flavor was unquestionably democratic, and the democratic cry had been raised lustily in behalf of free lands and protective tariffs and against the national bank. But little had been said about the oppression and inequality which characterized the factory system rising in the northeastern corner of the nation. There, little children toiled from sun to sun in miserable factory buildings, wages were scarcely sufficient to keep body and soul together, and the control of the capitalist was unrestrained except as paternalism might interfere. Native workers were being slowly crowded aside by the newly arrived foreigners, who were willing to accept the growing impersonality of the industrial system. New and greater wealth passed into fewer hands as merchant and industrial capitalism matured and a more powerful aristocracy than America had ever known took its place at the head of northern society. As little was said about Negro slavery which was taking a new hold on the greater South rising with the spread of cotton. Black families, condemned by the chance of birth to perpetual bondage, toiled long hours and suffered as much of abuse as Christian masters might be inclined to inflict. Southern men talked of the planter corresponding to the nobility of Europe. If these things had anything to do with the democracy which had come in with the rise of the new West, no one seemed conscious of the fact.

III

DEMOCRACY AND THE CIVIL WAR

✲

ON THE battlefield at Gettysburg in November, 1863, Abraham Lincoln asserted the democratic purpose of the war between the states. The North was fighting, he said, to preserve a "new nation, conceived in Liberty, and dedicated to the proposition that all men are created equal." He seemed to think that it was worth saving only because it was "so conceived and so dedicated." Victory for the North would mean "a new birth of freedom" and the continuation of "government of the people, by the people, for the people."

This fight to save democracy on the American continent, however, brought strange results. A few years after the war was ended, and as a direct result of it, the Supreme Court "abdicated" and refused to perform its part in the balance of government. The president of the United States was impeached, and a tyrannical, parliamentary form of government under Congress was instituted. An industrial interest, fattening on privilege, dominated the life of the nation and reduced the South and West to a position which Professor Walter P. Webb in a recent book calls "dependency." One portion of the nation was occupied by an army for some ten years after peace had been declared, and was denied self-rule while that army supported self-seeking outsiders and Negroes, just out of slavery, in office and plunder. Such were the returns on the nation's greatest investment in democracy!

How can we explain such an outcome? How did it happen that a great war of sacrifice for democracy almost put an end to what little democracy we already had? The answer can be found only in a clearer understanding of the forces actually at work in producing that war and in giving it the character which it took.

Historians have offered a wide variety of explanations for the coming of the war between the states. Contemporaries and those who wrote immediately after the struggle were inclined to talk about the North having been settled by Puritans who lived in a stimulating climate on stingy soils and builded a unique civilization, and Cavaliers who settled the South, enjoyed its mellow climate, and produced a way of life so different from that of the North that a war was necessary to see which one of them had to be abolished.

This is a simple and comfortable explanation. It has, however, one very serious fault: it is not true. The peoples who settled Massachusetts and New York were of exactly the same blood and station as those who went to Virginia and North Carolina. The myth of Puritan and Cavalier has long since been completely exploded. Furthermore, in spite of a warmer climate, a heavier rainfall, and a longer growing season, the South does not constitute a separate, distinct climatic province. There are only two tropical spots within its borders—one in Texas and one in Florida. Its extremes of heat and cold are comparable to those of the Middle West—the high marks of Iowa and Indiana seldom being reached in Georgia or Tennessee, and persons having been frozen to death in every southern state. The men of the South who followed Lee to Gettysburg were exactly the same in blood and ideals as their fathers who had entered into the "more perfect Union" formed at Philadelphia, and as their sons and grandsons who today live contentedly under the same government with the North. Their differences in 1861 were not inherent, basic differences born of separate origins.

Later explanations of the coming of civil war between the sections have emphasized the growth of distinct economic differences in the North and the South. The one was commercial, then industrial; its rural peoples were mostly farmers producing for domestic markets. As time went on industrial capitalism more and more dominated the section and insisted on sound finances, protective tariffs, homesteads, cheap foreign labor, and a more active government. The other was always an agricultural region where staple crops were produced for foreign markets. The plantation, with division and supervision of labor (in this case Negro labor, working under a system called slavery), played an important part in its economy. It needed free trade, local control of domestic institutions, easy credit, and cared little for cheap lands in the West to which its people would not go, or for the foreign immigrant who avoided

71

the section where Negroes already occupied the lower levels of society.

These historians see an economic rivalry which brought the sections into increasing conflict over legislation and then into a contest for power in the territories of the West. They believe that the institution of slavery became tangled with the sectional quarrel because the South could count three-fifths of its workers as population when representation in Congress was apportioned, even though they were held as property, and because slavery constituted a vulnerable spot in the armor of a rival for favorable legislation. They see the doctrines of consolidation and states' rights used by the contending parties to further their separate ends, and appeals to the Constitution made in differing ways to suit differing interests. They find a gradual emotionalizing of differences, the growth of fears and apprehensions, and, in the end, the drift of events out of control when a little blood was spilled. They are not certain whether it was a repressible conflict or an irrepressible one. George Fort Milton has called it "the needless war."

To accept either of these points of view does

not help us much to understand what democracy had to do with the struggle unless we assume, as Lincoln did, that one side had a monopoly of the national supply of freedom and equality and all the other things which had to do with justice and well-being. Contemporaries about to begin the killing of their fellows might be expected to assume that; but we ought to be far enough away from the passions of that day to know that this was not the case and to view the whole affair as a national tragedy. If we would understand the part played by the democratic dogma in this bitter struggle, we must range widely and forget the assertions of excited contemporaries. We must begin our search in New England in the days when the factory made its appearance.

The Industrial Revolution, which had already remade parts of western Europe, came to the United States gradually through the years following the War of 1812. It was confined, in the beginning, largely to southern New England, with Massachusetts and Rhode Island as its centers. Early efforts were carried on in simple fashion. Much work was done in the home, and the central establishment arose large-

ly to finish and market the raw materials put
out and fashioned by thrifty rural families.
Only gradually did the factory come. Capital
long invested in shipping did not shift easily,
and marketing rather than actual manufacturing of goods consumed the time and the efforts
of the entrepreneurs. New England farmers,
who had never found a profitable surplus or
large markets for the few things they produced,
were thus enabled to supplement the yield of
their stony acres by the weaving and spinning
of yarns or the sewing and pegging of shoes.
Wives and children found new employment and
prepared themselves to follow industry down
into the factory when it appeared along some
neighboring stream.

Gradually a new and greater interest came
to the section. The fall line outdistanced the
harbor; youth found its opportunity in industry; wealth came to those who manufactured
goods and projected new enterprises. The industrial town came to New England as it had
earlier come to Old England, and the masters of
the loom began to dictate the policies of the
legislatures. By 1845 industry had matured to
the point where weaker concerns had been

largely crowded out and consolidation and growth had made a few companies dominant in the field. Labor had become conscious of the long hours and the hard working conditions and the meager pay received; strikes and lockouts were an accepted part of the new order. After 1845 native workers in large numbers left the factories. The foreign immigrant, until now largely employed at hard manual labor or in the kitchens, took their places in the mills. The Industrial Revolution had wrought its miracles and brought its troubles to one section of the American nation.

Alongside these changes, the rural life of the Northeast had also undergone rapid alteration. With the rise of the factory towns new markets were opened for both foodstuffs and raw materials. Favorably located lands were given over to specialized crops, and capital found its way into agriculture. Garden produce, dairy products, beef cattle, and sheep showed marked increases, and markets, like that at Brighton, near Boston, were crowded with larger and better supplies. Travelers noted the improved appearance of farms. Agricultural societies and agricultural periodicals appeared to preach improved methods and to indicate that it paid to improve. The regions immediately around the industrial towns showed the most marked effects, but farther out in the interior the feeding of stock and inclosing for sheep pastures changed the face of the countryside. By 1835 it was stated that one-third of the people in Vermont had become shepherds and the farmers of western Massachusetts had become so engrossed with their cattle and sheep that they were buying all their flour from New York. An agricultural revolution had gone along with the rise of industry. Free enterprise, the boast of American democracy, was yielding new dividends!

These great changes, however, had not been made without suffering. The land of "steady habits" could not be so violently altered without paying a price. The shift of capital and influence from the old commercial and fishing centers produced bitter resentments. As Boston absorbed the commerce of the section and became the financial center for both industry and commerce, Salem and Beverly and Newburyport distrusted and hated her even more than they did the equally prosperous city of New

York. When their more influential families migrated to Beacon Hill and began to intermarry with the new industrial aristocracy revolt was direct and open. They went so far as to vote the Democratic ticket. Professor A. B. Darling has pictured the anger and defiance of the weakening seacoast towns as their lesser crafts rocked in the wake of the great ships outbound from Boston, "Hub of the Universe." Colonel Henry Lee has told of the "mercantile *émigrés*" who "came up from Newburyport to Boston, social and kindly people, inclined to make acquaintances and mingle with the world pleasantly. But [they] got some Cabot wives, who shut them up."

The rise of the factory and the development of an industrial order brought more of blessings to the capitalist than to the laborers. In early days children made up an unusually large percentage of the workers. From 1800 to 1860 they comprised from two- to three-fifths of the total. In 1825 the *Mechanics Free Press* declared that it was a "well-known fact that the principal part of the help in cotton factories consists of boys and girls . . . . from six to seventeen years of age . . . . confined to steady employment during the longest days of the year, from daylight until dark, allowing at the outside one hour and a half [for meals] . . . . and that too with a small sum that is hardly sufficient to support nature, while they [the employers] . . . . are rolling in wealth off the vitals of these poor children. . . . ." The same observer declared that the children were "as ignorant as Arabs of the desert"—not more than one-sixth of them being able to read or write. The "length of actual labor [in 1832]," says Professor R. T. Ely, "varied from twelve to fifteen hours." The New England mills generally ran thirteen hours, but one mill in Connecticut ran fourteen hours, while the mill at Griswold kept its machines turning fifteen hours and ten minutes per day. "Women and children were urged on by the use of the cowhide," he adds. Summing up the factory situation, Professors Carman and McKee of Columbia University write:

Living in miserable germ-infested quarters, laboring from sunrise to sunset for a wage that was a mere pittance, in factory buildings usually unfit to harbor a human being, many of these factory families led a pitiable existence. They were paid at irregular intervals, often not weekly or even monthly, and then frequently in depreciated or worthless money. Unemployment, debt, imprisonment, hunger, vice, drunkenness, sickness, and misery were the danger shoals upon which many were wrecked. . . . .[1]

Nor did the changes in agriculture work out much better. Specialization of crops and the wide use of capital by the few either sent a first wave of rural New Englanders toward the west, where they could continue to raise old crops in the old ways, or drove them into the towns as factory workers. The building of railways into the interior of the section widened the opportunities for the new agriculture and forced others along the same paths. Then the railroads reached across the Berkshires into New York, whose lands were more fertile and whose agricultural production was more abundant. New England farmers who had just expanded to take advantage of the new markets found competition in some lines too strong . They had to shift crops and many failed. As wheat, the first great frontier crop, continued to move westward into Ohio, then Michigan, Indiana, Illinois, and Wisconsin, farmers all along the line were forced to alter their production. First the Erie Canal and later the railroad carried in-

[1] Harry J. Carman and Samuel McKee, Jr., *A History of the United States* (Boston: D. C. Heath, 1931), I, 542–43.

creasing quantities of all kinds of agricultural produce back toward the coast where the new factory markets attracted. Slowly the New England farmer was crowded out of sheep and cattle production, then out of the dairy, then in large part out of gardening and fruit production. Only in favored spots and in the most perishable of produce could he compete. As a New England agricultural paper said: "It is perfectly evident that farmers, with moderate means, must go down by the thousands. And what is infinitely the most to be regretted, they go down in poverty." Under such conditions, thousands turned toward the factory towns to become industrial workers; thousands trekked westward to begin over again along the Great Lakes, where a "greater New England," as Dr. Turner calls it, was coming into being. Abandoned farms appeared all over the section. The foreigner took to farming in a more highly specialized and restricted way. Rural New England entered a new era in which her old independent farmers, like the lesser industrialists and the old commercial centers, lost their place and importance.

Those who left New England soon found

their condition little better than that of those who stayed at home. The industrial movement and the changing character of commerce were not confined alone to New England. They spread down into the lower part of New York, across into New Jersey, and toward Philadelphia. To the Yankee textiles and shoes these regions added iron manufacturing, and an even stronger pressure for tariffs than came from New England. Their workers often preceded those of the farther North in organization and in protest against the evils of industry. The farmers, especially of upper New York, specialized for these markets as well as for those of New England, and they in turn felt the competition from the farther West as transportation, usually financed by the industrial groups, reached farther and farther into the interior in quest of markets and supplies. In the 1830's they gave up wheat to a large degree, took over cattle and sheep, and found opportunities in the dairy. In the forties and fifties they were even crowded in some measure from these lines and a heavy emigration set in toward the cheaper and better lands of the farther west. Poverty and ruin fell on those who remained behind. Aban-

doned farms characterized the New York countryside as much as they did that of New England.

In the forties farmers of upper New York, of
Ohio, and of Michigan were organizing anti-
corn-law leagues in the hope of opening British
markets for their grain, and complaining that
their crops had stood in the fields unharvested
for the past seven years. To make matters
worse, legislation to give cheaper lands, to improve the western rivers and the lake harbors,
to open markets abroad failed because of southern opposition. Tariffs to help home markets
and to bring factories and diversification to
their sagging economic life also failed for the
same reason. Democracy was not looking after
the lesser folks for whom the government had
been founded. Powerful interests, resident in
other hands, controlled the parties which Andrew Jackson had taught Americans how to
use. Something very serious was wrong with
the whole system.

To these ills within the North and upper
Northwest was being added another by the
growth of Negro slavery in the South. The
spread of the "Kingdom of Cotton" to the deep

South had given the peculiar institution new strength and new importance. Cotton, rice, sugar, and tobacco, raised with slave labor, constituted by far the greater proportion of the nation's exports. The cotton planter rivaled the industrialist in wealth and position. The South in alliance with the older West in Tennessee and the Ohio Valley gained control of the Democratic party, and the Democratic party took charge of the central government to shape legislation according to the wishes of these agricultural regions. The second national bank was destroyed and all efforts to re-establish it failed; the tariff was lowered and kept going lower with each succeeding measure; the government showed itself interested in cotton markets and in protecting the interests of the slaveholders, but seemed to care little whether wheat found good markets, or whether industry in the United States prospered or not. The rivers and harbors of the North along the Great Lakes could not be improved while southerners interposed a strict construction of the Constitution as a barrier.

Such neglect caused some men to say that there was a slave power in America, aristocratic and domineering. Its extravagances in building great houses and in luxurious living, and its inability and dishonesty in meeting obligations, were plunging the nation into panics and ruining those who lived in New England, New York, or Ohio. Its defiance of democracy in holding slaves prevented America from fulfilling its great destiny. Here was even stronger evidence of democracy's failure. Here was another field for humanitarian effort.

Such foundations for resentments and revolt had never before existed in any part of the United States. All that men here and elsewhere have objected to in the factory, the machine, and the industrial capitalist were to be found— the abuse of labor, especially that of children and women; unsanitary working conditions; the tyranny of machines; the harsh materialism of an industrial order; the power of those with capital. To it had been added all the bitterness of an agricultural order attempting to adjust itself to the town and factory and to competition with a rising West. And just beyond, peopled by those who had first experienced the ills of industry, was another West, disillusioned and complaining, certain that others were responsible for its failure to prosper and quickly to leave pioneer conditions behind. All of it moved on a stern Puritan background, which insisted on the mission to achieve a holy commonwealth and was characterized by the unending urge in every man to become his brother's keeper. Something new and something greater for American democracy had to come from such a situation.

Revolt began early. Sometimes it took the form of protest against existing abuses. Sometimes it consisted of sharp criticism of the drift toward greater interdependence, of the livelihood of so many people in the control of the few, of the emphasis upon material values. Again it expressed itself in fantastic schemes by which perfection of society could be achieved. One writer characterized it as "a day of ideals in every camp," of "high-flying souls," of a "keener scrutiny of institutions and domestic life." James Russell Lowell laughingly spoke of "every possible form of intellectual and physical dyspepsia" bringing forth its gospel. He chided those who stressed plainness of speech and dress, the use of hooks and eyes in place of buttons, and who formed "communities where everything was to be common but common sense." But even he recognized the fact that back of all this stirring lay deep, fundamental forces which would smash sacred things to pieces unless changes soon were made.

Out of the general stirring came a whole series of well-organized reform movements. One sought to end the evils of intemperance; another denounced war and struggled to bring peace to mankind throughout the earth; a third aimed at giving woman her rights; a fourth to secure intelligent treatment of the criminal and the insane. Others attempted to improve the lot of common men by public education and a wider distribution of government lands. At Brook Farm, at Fruitlands, at New Harmony, and at other places high-flying souls tried to put into practice their notions of a better social order and a more just allotment of goods and labor. Back of each of these movements was a democratic impulse, often vaguely expressed and tangled with other drives. But the feeling that certain things did not belong in America and that this nation had a higher destiny to fulfil was strong in every movement. The urge to check privilege was nearly as great. Faith in the perfectibility of the individual and a willingness to work to set him free for the achievement of a higher individual destiny were generally the dominating characteristics.

As part and parcel of these reform movements came the northern antislavery crusade. It had its origins in the same seedbed; its leaders and the membership of the organizations formed to forward its course were identical with those of temperance, woman's rights, peace, etc. There was nothing unusual about it in the beginning to indicate that it would be of any greater importance than the others. Gradually, however, antislavery forged to the front and soon crowded other efforts aside. By 1850 it had become the North's great reform movement and the carrier of its humanitarian impulses. The reasons for this will be noted later. For the present it is sufficient to remember that the northern crusade against southern slavery began as part of a larger humanitarian drive which would end a host of evils that had come to plague a section.

It should also be noticed that most of these reform efforts represented the interests of an upper class and touched the workers and farmers only to a slight degree. The New England clergy, the intellectuals, and a few prominent businessmen took the lead and found a following among persons of their own class and interests. Those who directly felt the evils of the new day took little part. Working men and farmers had neither time nor inclination for abstract reform. Immediate realities were too pressing.

These groups, however, were not passive. When they began to act, their expressions went directly to the heart of the whole matter. Democracy was being destroyed and, while intemperance and other evils might need checking, the call was for something much more fundamental. Aristocrats must be pulled down. The rights of common men must be respected and steps taken to insure a greater equality. They would launch a true democratic crusade to rescue America from the new forces which threatened to destroy the great purposes for which it had been founded.

Without attempting to distinguish clearly between the attitudes shown in the farmers' movement in Massachusetts, the workingmen's movement in New York City or Philadelphia, and the "locofoco" groups in upper and western New York, we must notice that the resentments were sometimes those of the poor against the rich, sometimes those of the country people against the towns, and sometimes those of the many against the privileges of the few. Everywhere the appeal was to democracy against aristocracy as an American right.

In 1836 *Niles' Weekly Register* commented on "the feeling of envy and even hatred [which] seem[ed] to be in persons as strong as those of the serfs of Europe against the privileged classes," and defended those who had acquired wealth in the United States on the ground that it had been done by dint of hard labor. The *New England Farmer* spoke of the "ruinous debts and mortgages" which were due to "the excessive accumulations of property in the hands of a limited number of individuals" and urged the people to awaken and to "devise some efficient remedy." A plain farmer wrote of "the industry on the part of the farmers and pleasure on the part of the aristocracy" and another declared that we had reached the point where we talked about political equality "as we would discourse of the millennium," and accounted it a "subject of hope rather than of present fruition." He spoke of the few who by their wealth were in a position to make hewers of wood and drawers of water out of their fellows and begged that he and his wife be spared from the humiliation of performing servile offices, or his children from working in the kitchens of his "more fortunate neighbors." The working-men's movement in Massachusetts was, says Professor Darling, a protest against domination by the accumulators in Boston and the exclusive privileges of the wealthy who controlled the banks and other corporations.

The mechanics of Philadelphia, asserting that they were "conscious that [their] condition in society [was] lower than justice demanded it should be," and realizing that they could not individually ward off the numerous evils which resulted from the unequal and very excessive accumulations of wealth and power in the hands of the few, determined to organize into a labor union for mutual protection. Fanny Wright described the movement in New York city as ". . . . a war of classes. It was the ridden people who were making common cause against oppression, and struggling to throw from their backs the booted and spurred riders whose legitimate title to starve as well as to work them to death will no longer pass current. . . . ." "Are we who confer almost every blessing on society, never to be treated as free men and equals?" asked one group of workers. "Is it equitable that we should waste the energies of our minds and bodies, and be placed in a situation of such unceasing exertion and servility as must necessarily in time render the benefits of our liberal institutions to us inaccessible and useless, in order that the products of our labour may be accumulated by a few into vast pernicious masses, calculated to prepare the minds of the possessors for the exercise of lawless rule and despotism to overawe the meagre multitude and fright away the shadow of freedom which still lingers among us?" A new sharing of the public lands, of the benefits of education, and of the returns of production were necessary if America were to fulfil its destiny.

This movement reached its climax in the rural sections of upper and western New York, in what is sometimes called the "locofoco" movement, the most remarkable democratic effort ever staged on the American continent.

Its leaders went back to the Declaration of Independence and then turned to the Bible, weaving and blending them into a common body of doctrine to justify a social reordering of things as they were and an effort to set America on the course which it was intended in the beginning it should follow. Here, with these simple country people, was the beginning of the doctrines which would make war between North and South inevitable and give whatever of democratic significance that war was to have.

"These Methodists of Democracy," said one of their leaders, "introduced no new doctrines, no new articles, into the true creed; they only revived those heaven-born principles which had been so long trodden under the foot of Monopoly and forgotten that they were termed 'the new-fangled notions of Loco-focoism.'" Just what this meant was shown by another writer who said:

For Democracy is the cause of Humanity. It has faith in human nature. It believes in its essential equality and fundamental goodness. . . . . Its object is to emancipate the mind of the masses of men from the degrading and disheartening fetters of social distinctions and advantages . . . . by striking at their root to reform all the infinitely varied human misery which has grown out of the old and false ideas by which the world has been so long misgoverned; to dismiss the hireling soldier; to spike the cannon, and bury the bayonet; to burn the gibbet, and open the debtor's dungeon; to substitute harmony and mutual respect for the jealousies and discord now subsisting between different classes of society, as the consequence of their artificial classification. It is essentially involved in Christianity, of which it has been well said that its pervading spirit of democratic equality among men is its highest fact. . . . .

From a practical angle one of its speakers declared that "at present, although we may live under the cloak of republicanism we are in reality subjected to the worst of all tyrannies— an aristocracy of wealth. Our actual government, our real regulator of social rights and social intercourse, is money—the greater heaps ruling the less. . . . ." To which text another added the comment: "It ought ever to be borne in mind, that no man can acquire the doubtful good of extreme wealth without subjecting others to the undoubted evil of poverty. No man can gain the whole soil of a district without stripping all the other occupants of such district of their right to the soil; nor engross any portion of the fruits of other men's labor without subjecting others to a loss equal to his own gain. Hence, no doubt, the severity of the denunciations pronounced by the carpenter of Nazareth upon the engrossers of wealth; who in the very nature of things, ever must be little better than beasts of prey lying in wait for the honest laborers of society. . . . ."

Over and over again they paraphrased the Declaration of Independence, asserting their belief "that all men are created equal, and endowed by their Creator with certain inalienable rights"; as often they found the same doctrine in Christianity. The historian of the movement dedicates his volume "To a Believer who has rejoiced in the light of Locofocoism, as an outward sign of the inward light of Christianity. . . . ."

All this may seem a long way from the Civil War. In fact it is the very heart of the whole struggle, in so far as it had to do with democracy. The combination of democracy and Christianity for the destruction of social evils and the realization of America's destiny provided the attitudes and forces which were soon to be turned solidly against slavery and the South. Out of the thinking generated to meet the ills of industry and farming was to come the basic doctrines with which a rival section and its institutions would be struck down in the name of democracy and Christianity. Here was the idea that God had created a moral law for human government and endowed man with a conscience with which to apprehend it. Our Constitution, our law, was intended to approximate that fundamental law; American society was intended to be a moral society. Where the Constitution or legislation fell short of what man's conscience told him was right, then there was a "higher law" to which appeal might be made. In practice the individual was under no obligation to obey the unjust law or to respect the undemocratic constitutional principle.

Here was a new individualism, a new freedom for the just man who rose above government because he was in step with the "law of the Universe," as Emerson called it. Here, too, was the basic notion that God was particularly interested in the American social order as his own great experiment in government.

If the democratic doctrine upheld such thinking, Christianity gave equal support. The all-powerful God of the Calvinists, whose unbending will ruled the universe, served the same purpose as the democratic moral law; conversion and freedom from sin stripped the individual naked before his God and put him in step with the divine will; the Christian millennium, already expected daily in rural New York, fell in perfectly with the democratic notion of a perfect order to be achieved for the glory of God on the American continent.

Armed with such doctrines the Puritan could brook no interference. His prosperity and his quick realization of advancement were one with the will and purposes of God. Resistance was of the devil; opponents were aristocrats. Foes could not plead their constitutional rights nor depend on the protection of the law. The world was a battlefield; there could be no peace until God's will, as understood by his chosen, ruled the everyday affairs of men.

With these things in mind we need only to recall the sharp development of sectional rivalry which characterized the years from 1830 to 1860. It was basically a rivalry between a staple producing agricultural region and a commercial-industrial one, with the West as a third section sometimes siding with the South and sometimes with the North. In a very broad sense the contending parties differed in their conception of government's proper part in developments—the North tending to favor consolidation or broad use of powers and the South inclined to support strict construction of the Constitution and local control of affairs. But for our purposes the significant part about these developments was the fact that around 1844 the politicians, in their struggle for personal and sectional interests, began to make use of the slavery issue—which until then had belonged to the professional reformers. In a concrete sense they were struggling over tariffs, homesteads, river and harbor improvements, railways, and the organization of new territories. Yet because the South opposed these things and the North and West favored them, and the South had slaves and the North did not, the struggle was soon cast in terms of slavery versus freedom. Slavery became the symbol of the whole southern way of life, its interest and values. Freedom symbolized the North and its interests and values. Neither symbol carried a correct impression of the realities behind it. Three-fourths of the southern people had no connection whatever with slavery; thousands of northern men and women knew little of freedom from want and oppression. In this way the false notion grew up that the South, as a slave interest, controlled the Democratic party, which in turn ruled the nation, prevented the passage of all legislation favorable to the North and West, and passed all measures favorable to the South. Thus the "slave power" tyrannized over the North and checked the growth of truly democratic living. The southern defense of its institution strengthened the impression by praising a stratified society and denouncing, as "false and foolish," the Declaration of Independence. The interests of the white worker as well as those of the Negro were at stake. That fact took the slavery issue away from the professional reformer and turned it over to the politician; it made slavery the outstanding evil of the day; opposition to slavery the purpose of every honest man.

This can be seen in the comments made in the North on the various sectional issues of the period. When Texas was annexed and the tariff of 1846 passed with its two senators voting in its favor, Joshua Giddings exclaimed: "Are the liberty-loving democrats of Pennsylvania ready to give up the tariff? To strike off all protection from the articles of iron and coal and other productions of that state, in order to purchase a slave market for their neighbors who . . . . breed men for the market like oxen for the shambles?" And when the river-and-harbor bill was vetoed by President Polk, a Chicago paper declared that the "lives and property of the freemen of the North, her laborers, sailors, and those passing to and fro upon her Great Lakes and Rivers" lived "in a portion of the country which was out of the pale and care" of the government under southern control. It ended its statement by saying that

the North can and will be no longer hoodwinked. If no measures for the protection and improvement of anything North are to be suffered by our Southern masters, if we are to be downtrodden, and all our cherished interests crushed by them, a signal revolution will inevitably ensue. The same spirit and energy that forced emancipation for the whole country from Great Britain will throw off the Southern yoke. . . . . Southern rule is at an end.

When the territorial dispute developed over California and New Mexico, William H. Seward, from the old locofoco district of New York, declared that slavery was a sin and Americans could not "be either true Christians or real freemen, if they imposed on another a chain they defied all human power to fasten on themselves." The American conscience was against the South, he said. Human law "must be brought to the standard of the law of God. . . . ." The Constitution did not "recognize property in man" and if it did "there was a higher law than the Constitution." The North had taken over in its entirety for its fight against the South the old doctrine of the revolting workers and farmers of the earlier period.

To complete the picture it was necessary to depict the South as a land of aristocrats and immoral people. The southern people, they charged, were descendants of Cavaliers; they lived in great white-pillared houses in luxury and extravagance surrounded by black servants who attended their slightest whim; they spent their days in idleness and dissipation; they drank excessively; they indulged in cruel cock fights and horse racing; the average southern home was little better than a "brothel," where unrestrained sexual irregularity at the expense of black women filled the section with mulattoes. The South took the place of all the enemies of democracy and Christianity which had once been found at home.

With the birth of the Republican party as the carrier of northern demands in homesteads, tariffs, Pacific railroads, and other economic interests of the section, that party became by necessity and inference the party of both democracy and morality. It found in the end as its great leader a man who phrased its purposes as carrying forward "the eternal struggle between right and wrong" and the forwarding of the government "of the people, by the people, for the people." When war came he turned it into a struggle to preserve the Union, which actually meant the old New England holy commonwealth.

When that war was over and hundreds of thousands of men had laid down their lives and millions of dollars had been spent, it was discovered that the actual results of victory had been the triumph of industry over agriculture; of centralization over local democracy; of one section over another; of the Republican party, representing bourgeois acquisitiveness, over its Democratic rival, representing an older agrarian ideal. Industrial capitalism was in the saddle and the urban world was to set the patterns for a new America. Even the democratic Lincoln would become the figurehead of a political party dedicated to the advancement of a thoroughly undemocratic industrial and finance capitalism. As a new national symbol of the democratic faith he would henceforward help to satisfy the American desire to render lip service to democracy while freedom and equality were being trampled under foot in the greedy drive for wealth and place.

IV

DEMOCRACY AND INDUSTRIAL
CAPITALISM

✳

UNTIL the Civil War, agriculture was
the dominant interest in the United
States. The great majority of the people lived in rural areas and thought and valued
things much as Thomas Jefferson believed that
farmers should do. Life was more or less simple; the average level of well-being remarkably
high. A liberal land policy had enabled what
might have been "poor folks" elsewhere to get
a start and the force of the frontier had kept
down those who might in other lands have assumed a superior social rank. Common men,
given freedom in the presence of great natural
resources generously opened to them, were
writing a new chapter in the history of mankind. European travelers commented on the
high average of comfort and even luxury; they
noted the lack of subservience in demeanor;
they were astonished at the few paupers and at

the absence of organized charity. America was still the "land of opportunity." The rapid growth of slums and the generally low levels at which the recently arrived immigrants lived and worked did not invalidate the larger fact. The savage grasping of the speculator, the harsh indifference of the factory owners, the hard driving of Negro slaves in cotton fields, only emphasized the fact that most men prospered according to their willingness to toil, to save, and to sacrifice. America was also "the land of plenty."

Equally important was the meaning which these Americans gave to the word "plenty." When they used the term they usually meant that there were enough to eat, enough to wear, and a sufficiency in shelter; that the children were in school, and that, in addition to the everyday clothing which they had on, there was a Sunday dress or suit in the closet at home; that they were able to go a-visiting at intervals, attend the circus when it came to town once a year, take in the church and school festivals, and have grandfather's portrait enlarged in charcoal when the traveling artist came around.

In 1840 there was published in New York City a list of all citizens who were considered to be wealthy. It is interesting to notice that the list included men whose property was valued at only fifty thousand dollars and that the greater percentage ranged around one hundred thousand dollars. There were only a few millionaires in the whole country; John Jacob Astor's twenty-five millions topped the list.

Away from the seaboard, wealth consisted of the ownership of a farm, a store, a professional education, and the good health with which to make a living from them. Luxury was implied in travel, a horse and buggy, a Brussels carpet, an organ, and a dish of bananas and oranges on the dining-room table at all times. Vacations were hardly known, amusements were in the home, the church, or the school. The wider spending of money on self-indulgence was more or less related to sinfulness. Men and women worked hard and long; children had their chores. The home supplied its own bread, butter, meat, and vegetables. Leisure was quite unknown.

With the Civil War and the so-called Reconstruction period, all this changed rapidly. A series of events, almost revolutionary in character, crowded the old America aside and began to usher in the modern age. In the first place the Old South, which had played so important a part in the life of the nation up to the Civil War, was bitterly crushed and thrust aside. By 1865 thousands of productive citizens had been killed or maimed; great stretches of territory had been invaded and left in smoking ruins; once fertile fields were galled and gullied; government had collapsed and a "cause" for which men had been willing to go to war had been lost. One section of the nation, whose total wealth in 1860 was about three and one-third billions of dollars, had in 1865 a debt of over two and one-half billions—every cent of which was to be absolutely repudiated, along with some sixty-seven millions of state debts. Furthermore, a large proportion of that section's capital had been invested in slaves, which were now freed without compensation of any kind. The South was literally bankrupt.

For years to come the once dominant spokesman of agricultural interests in the United States could play only a minor role in national affairs. Her interests would be primarily local

106

and her energies consumed in her own social-economic recovery. A pressing race question would rob her of the benefits of the two-party system and necessity would make her into a "solid South" unable politically to express her varied opinions on varied problems. For decades the South would be a section where the farmers, the unorganized laborers, and the Negroes—the three great exploited groups in America—would predominate. The old plantation system would give way to tenantry and share-cropping; virtual peasantry would take the place of gentility in agriculture. The South in modern America would be forced to practice what Jonathan Daniels has called "the economy of want."

But war and reconstruction did even more drastic things to the North and West. It brought the Industrial Revolution, which had already transformed the Northeast, to a rapid and unrestricted completion, and made modern America dominantly urban-industrial. The war itself gave the first real push. It called for goods and men at the same time and brought the machine to control. Manufacturing boomed. With the South, as the opponent of industry and of the legislation necessary for its most rapid expansion, out of the way, industrial capitalism could sweep forward without restraint or criticism. The control of government was in its hands; public opinion, now reinforced with patriotism, was behind it. Quickly the homestead bill was passed, tariffs were moved upward, a national banking law was put in force, and the doors were swung open to immigration. Huge and profitable war contracts went to industry; the floating of enormous war loans was turned over to the bankers. Wealth piled up as it had never done before in America; the industrial belt widened to include centers well scattered over the North; a new group rose to control in American life.

The war, moreover, brought a basic change in construction materials. The old order had been one of wood and brick and stone. Now came the age of iron and steel. America had to be rebuilt as well as saved. The job was a factory job. The machine would do the work. Production limits were fixed only by capacity. Prices could be set at almost any level.

Under such conditions the North felt the war

only as a stimulant. With all the fighting, all the young men engaged in the work of destruction, the section drove forward in production and expansion at a rate never dreamed of in the earlier decades. It came out of war into peace far stronger than it had entered. After 1865 it was ready to go ahead into the greatest period of industrial development any people on the face of the earth had ever known. The years from Appomattox to the end of the nineteenth century were to be the age of big business.

Many factors favored this development. First and most important was the American market. Rapid urban growth and an even more rapid expansion into the West called for increasing quantities of supplies for building, for transportation, and for consumption. The standards of living were high; the purchasing power greater than that of any other peoples in the world. The average American consumed proportionately more of the new things which industry was creating than even the privileged few of the older countries. He built and he tore down before he could wear out. He tried new things; he talked about the American standard of living as though it were his most prized possession. And this matchless American market was monopolized for the American manufacturer by extravagant tariffs, passed for war needs often without intelligent debate, and then left untouched or even increased in days of peace. No wonder that the earnings of one year sometimes equaled or surpassed the original capital invested in a concern.

To this advantage was added another of almost equal importance. The great natural resources of earth's richest continent were passed out freely under the homestead type of legislation to those who would use them. Millions of acres of fertile land were given to the railroads. The rich iron ores, the magnificent supplies of timber, the great stores of oil, quickly reached private hands. Here all the materials for the new age were to be found in abundance such as no other single continent, let alone a single nation, could boast. At a minimum price they belonged to those who were in a position to exploit them. With all the disadvantages of waste and high labor costs, the American industrialist was soon underselling all competitors in the open markets of the world.

And as if this were not enough, the poor of

Europe poured into the country to give a comparatively cheap labor supply—even willing, on occasion, to be exploited as were the raw resources themselves. Not until the end of the century would Americans sympathize with them or believe their lot hard. What the Negro slave had been to the cotton South, foreign labor was to industry in the post–Civil War North.

Another favorable factor for industry was the American attitude toward these developments. Starting with a frontier in which agriculture was usually a first primitive effort, the average American was inclined to measure all advance in terms of industrial developments. The coming of the factory meant that progress was being made. It ought to be encouraged, even favored. Government gave lands and all the rich resources they contained; communities taxed themselves to grant favors; kindly intended persons approved of the exploitation of men and resources in the interests of new factories. The industrial capitalist was exalted above all others. His success in the accumulation of wealth was viewed as evidence of his matchless ability. He became the fountain of all knowledge, the keeper of the public good. The descriptions of Frick, Hill, Carnegie, Morgan, and their kind, given by enthusiastic biographers, are more like those of gods than of men. Joseph G. Pyle speaks of the lordship which the whole man Hill proclaimed and compares his abilities to those of Napoleon; George B. Harvey declares that the lines of Frick's torso were hardly less classical than those drawn of "Hercules by a student of the master Lysippus," and requires two national champions to describe his golf game. Carl Hovey insists that J. Pierpont Morgan's personality was of the Olympian order, incapable of doubt and indecision. Professor William E. Dodd once referred to these men as "Complex Jehovahs." The name seems to apply.

Along with this worship of the successful businessman went a contempt for the laborer. The American notion that any man "worth his salt" would rise, left no room for those permanently in overalls. True, men should start in a small way, but they should all reach the very top in time. The hired man was supposed ultimately to own the farm; the office boy was expected someday to head the factory, the section hand to become the president of the railroad. These attitudes favored capital as against labor and prevented the development of a balanced industrial situation. As Henry Clews wrote in 1878:

Strikes may have been justifiable in other nations but they are not justifiable in our country. The Almighty has made this country for the oppressed of other nations, and therefore this is the land of refuge . . . . and the hand of the laboring man should not be raised against it. . . . .

The *Chicago Tribune* expressed the same attitude in July, 1877, saying:

If these men [the B. & O. strikers] think they can't take the wages offered them, they can step out and let others take their places who feel that they can live upon the wage. . . . . If the company should reduce their wages to a cent a day, they have but one privilege in the premises. They have a right to ask for an increase, and, if the request is refused, they have the right to step out. . . . .

Even the courts held that it was "un-American" to pass legislation forcing the capitalist to pay his workers in stated ways. "It tends to degrade them as citizens by impeaching their ability to take care of themselves," said an Indiana judge.

What these conditions and attitudes produced in terms of goods, I need not tell you. All in all a situation more favorable for capitalistic expansion could hardly be imagined. They created machinery and power to run machinery to the point where men did not need to work long hours to supply all their needs—goods such as kings of old could not possess and cheap enough for the average man to possess them. The technical story reads like a fairy tale. Leisure was soon not only possible, it was necessary. Man power became a drug on the market; goods for comfort and luxury so abundant they threatened to smother a whole people. The word "plenty" lost its old meaning. A new extravagance entered American life to make its cities splendid beyond the dream of the early American farmer. Homes and furnishings and entertainments so elaborate and yet so lacking in taste that only the term "the gilded age" fitly describes the period. Millionaires and multimillionaires to be counted by the thousands; American heiresses marrying into European royalty; American businessmen calling on kings and presenting lavish presents to their queens; enormous gifts to endow universities to make them into centers of research as well as country clubs; the art treasures of the ages bought and stored in American homes and museums; travel and leisure and extravagance at one end and toil and poverty at the other. America had come of industrial age.

The least attractive side of the whole development was revealed in the oft-quoted remarks of one Frederick Townsend Martin:

The class I represent care nothing for politics. Among my people I seldom hear purely political discussions. When we are discussing pro and con the relative merits of candidates or the relative importance of political policies, the discussion almost invariably comes down to the question of business efficiency. We care absolutely nothing about statehood bills, pension agitation, waterway appropriations, "porkbarrels," states' rights, or any other political question, save inasmuch as it threatens or fortifies existing conditions. Touch the question of tariff, touch the issue of the income tax, touch the problem of railroad regulation or touch the most vital of all business matters, the question of general federal regulation of industrial corporations, and the people amongst whom I live my life become immediately rabid partisans. . . . . It matters not one iota what political party is in power or what President holds the reins of office. We are not politicians or public thinkers; we are the rich; we own America; we got it, God knows how, but we intend to keep it if we can by throwing all the tremendous weight of our support, our influence, our money, our political connections, our purchased senators, our hungry congressmen, our public-speaking demagogues into the scale against any legislature, any political platform, any presidential campaign that threatens the integrity of our estate. . . . .

These remarks seem smart and irrelevant until one learns that on January 1, 1930, 78 per cent of American business wealth (not including banking) was corporate wealth; that the two hundred largest corporations controlled about 49 per cent of all this corporate wealth and 38 per cent of all the business wealth; that in these two hundred corporations only 6 per cent of the wealth was controlled by those who owned one-half or more of the stock. Then we can understand that Martin was not just talking.

In this forward sweep of industrialization two groups failed to share sufficiently in the benefits and had not approved of the philosophy. The industrial worker found himself increasingly limited in his ability to function as an individual. He had little chance to say where and for whom he worked. He had to labor where the machines were and for those to whom the machines belonged. He quickly realized that capital, by its very nature, was organized, and that America had a permanent laboring class whether the public was willing to recognize the fact or not. Organization called for organization. "We but imitate the example of capital," said the workers, "for in all the multifarious branches of trade, capital has its combinations and, whether intended or not, it crushes the manly hopes of labor and tramples poor humanity into the dust."

But organization of labor met opposition. Most employers believed with A. S. Wheeler of Boston that "it is perfectly right for the wage earner to get all he can . . . . but after all, one inexorable law finally settles this as it does so many other economic questions, and that is the law of supply and demand." The *New York Herald* put it a little more bluntly in saying: "There is no abuse which may not be remedied here by the ballot in everyman's hand and the Bible in everyman's heart." The *New York Times* gave it another turn by commenting that strikes and boycotts were "un-American . . . . and show that those who employ them have no real conception of what American citizenship is or implies." All meant the same thing. Things were all right as they were and labor should remain as it was. Christian employers would do what was just and right.

The workers, nevertheless, formed their unions, and in 1877 and again in 1884 struck against the railroads and soon against the great industrial corporations. Capital opposed as an interference with property rights and the public generally sided with the capitalists. Workers were viewed as foreigners who still thought as Europeans. More than one person suggested that they should be dealt with as European governments would deal with them. "If the club of the policeman, knocking out the brains of the rioters, will answer, then well and good," said the *Independent* in an editorial on July 26, 1877. "But if it does not promptly meet the exigency, then bullets and bayonets, canister and grape, with no sham or pretence . . . . constitute the only remedy. . . . ." The *New York Herald* bitterly denounced the workers for acting on the "presumption that they had a moral, if not legal, right to a living as trainmen on the roads they served. But this is an entirely un-American presumption." It said: "No man is entitled to a living out of any calling here. If he can't make a living in one line it is his business to go at something else. To hold otherwise would be to make him a slave."

The second disgruntled group were the farmers of the West. Up until the Civil War the combination of western and southern farmers had dictated the major policies of the nation. But now they were divided. For four long years they had been arrayed in blue and gray against each other, and the G.A.R. and the politicians were not willing to let them forget that fact. The "bloody shirt" still had elections to be wrung out of it. So behind protective tariff walls of nearly 50 per cent the manufacturers converted America into an industrial nation with the support of northern farmers whose surpluses of wheat and corn were used, ironically enough, to settle the adverse balances of trade in the international markets. The grain farmer kept voting the "right" ticket even though he could not control the size of his crops according to world-needs, nor create through advertising the notion that his product was a unique and invaluable thing to be purchased in preference to rival products of the same kind.

This close alliance between the western farmer and the eastern industrialist did not at first seem to threaten disaster. By that combination the homestead act was passed and war markets were opened. In war days and immediately afterward a new era of agricultural expansion began, which brought into being the great trans-Mississippi kingdoms of wheat, cattle, sheep, and corn. The war popularized a whole series of agricultural machines—the steel plow, the corn planter, the two-horse cultivator, the mower, the reaper, the steam thresher—all invented earlier but not widely used until war made man power scarce on the farm. Peace turned loose thousands of restless men who came home to find their places filled and production of all kinds piling up without their assistance. The flat, fertile prairies called to them; the homestead law made lands available; machinery supplied the means; the railroads, hurried forward by war needs, promised a way to profitable markets. The result was one of America's epics.

In the whole history of the United States up to 1870, there had been incorporated into farms only 407,735,041 acres of land. In the three decades after 1870, more than 430,000,000 acres were added. One generation of men settled more land and turned more of it into farms than all their predecessors put together. The figures for improved lands are even more startling. In

1870 there were 188,920,099 acres classified as improved—the work of all the farmers of the nation since Jamestown. The next ten years after 1870 saw 95,849,943 acres (50 per cent) added, and the next three decades, the active life-span of one generation, saw 225,000,000 added. One generation of men had improved 37,000,000 more acres than all their predecessors. By 1900 there were 478,451,750 improved acres in the United States as against the 163,-000,000 of 1860!

Figures mean little, but the facts were that the settlement of Iowa, Minnesota, Kansas, Nebraska, the Dakotas, and all the great "Inland Empires" of the Rocky Mountain area, where wheat was to erect its kingdom, and all the plains and mountain areas where the kingdom of range cattle was to be established, was accomplished in one mad rush, which was more like the rush into mining areas than like the old movements by which the agricultural regions of the United States had been settled.

I can only suggest the accomplishments on these lands. With machinery best fitted to just such level regions; with scientific aids furnished by both the federal and the state governments (now efficient through the new agricultural colleges); with the railroads pouring new settlers in and giving help as well; these regions began to pour back into the lap of an astonished world veritable floods of food.

Range cattle, for years so abundant that they had been killed only for their hides, now streamed out of Texas to fatten on the rich grasses of the plains. Possession of a water hole gave control over wide areas of government land. The eager railroads carried the surpluses to Chicago, where new packing and preserving methods soon destroyed the local slaughterhouses of the land and then monopolized the national and soon the international meat markets. It was the cheapest way of producing meat the earth had ever known.

The story of wheat is even more spectacular. Where its average acreage from 1866 to 1875 was only twenty millions, it rose in the next decade to over thirty-four millions. Yields rose from 173,000,000 bushels in 1860 to 498,-000,000 in 1880 and to over 522,000,000 in 1900. Common men all over the Western world might now eat white bread and roast beef, once the food of kings.

Other things were in proportion, and I will quote only one writer, who sums up the situation by saying:

"Year after year came from widening acreage . . . . torrents of wheat, of pork, of cattle, of corn, swelling the channels of trade and spreading over the whole civilized world. Year after year, more and more freight cars creaked wearily with heavier and heavier loads to cities whose prosperity waxed higher and higher and higher. . . . ." The effect of this amazing agricultural development was, as is usually the case, the ruination of the farmer who carried it out. Wheat will illustrate. Sold in a world-market, prices were seriously affected in the eighties when India, Russia, and Australia entered the market in earnest, and when France, Germany, Italy, and Spain raised tariff walls against American wheat. Where in 1866–75 it had sold at $1.053 per bushel and in 1876–85 at $0.92, it fell to $0.673 in 1886–95 and to $0.62 by 1900. The yield increased two and a half times between 1870 and 1900, but the total value was less than half what it had been.

Cattle and sheep followed a like course. The overcrowding of the range, a series of hard win-

ters, and the cow days were gone—passing, as
Professor E. E. Dale has said, almost overnight.
From 1866 to 1878, corn prices fell 32 per cent,
wheat 42 per cent, cotton 58 per cent. Only the
price of farm machinery seemed to increase. By
1900, 31 per cent of the nation's farms were mort-
gaged, with averages in Michigan, Minnesota,
Wisconsin, Iowa, and Nebraska running from
45 to 53 per cent. Tenantry mounted as rapidly,
reaching 35.3 per cent in 1900. A steady stream
of enterprising boys and girls ran off from the
farms into the cities, the new lands of opportunity, excitement, and adventure. The last
independent farmers of the Old World, mean-
while, were slowly sinking to peasantry under
the flood of cheap American produce.

The reactions to these developments among
the workers and the farmers were of two kinds.
The first was in the form of sharp complaint
against the immediate hard times and the ills
which overexpansion, debts, railroad rates,
high rates of interest, low wages, mortgages,
etc., had produced. The second was a serious
questioning of the whole course which American life had taken. Men began to take stock of
the industrial age and to ask how the American

dream was faring, how democracy had come out in the mad rush to prosperity. A new protest group had been developed. It was time to talk about Thomas Jefferson again.

Henry George, walking the streets of New York in 1869, saw the sharp contrast between the brilliant extravagance of the rich and the numbing poverty of the poor. Fashionable residences rubbed shoulders with the slums. The gilded age of the industrial rich and the vice and want of the tenement districts revealed the inconsistency of progress and poverty. It did not make sense in democratic America. Back to the Declaration of Independence he went. "Insidious forces" were producing "inequality," destroying liberty. Either we must accept the full implications of freedom in the United States "or she will not stay." "It is not enough that men should vote," he said, "it is not enough that they should be theoretically equal before the law. They must have liberty to avail themselves of the opportunities and means of life; they must stand on equal terms with reference to the bounties of nature. Either this or Liberty withdraws her light! Either this or darkness comes on, and the very forces that progress has evolved turn to powers that work destruction." Poverty was not the result of a decree of God, a curse on man. It was a social evil which had no place in the good society. George found the great trouble in the fact that man's God-given right to the use of the earth had been denied by private ownership of the land which made some men bondsmen of others. By the single tax he would give new equality. The state might become an instrument through the taxing power by which freedom and equality might be actualities.

Edward Bellamy a little later faced the problem of happiness in a machine age, and reached the conclusion that the destroying competition of the new era was responsible for the great gap between what seemed possible and what really existed. He, too, turned back to Jefferson. "Equality is the vital principle of democracy," he said. Until we recognized the "worth and dignity of the individual" and made material conditions subservient to his well-being, democracy could not exist. He would inspire Americans to work for the good society. He would plan the economic life, the social life, so as to preserve the benefits of the machine and yet give a new equality and a new security to every man and woman and child.

Henry Lloyd struck even more savagely. He wrote:

Nature is rich, but everywhere man, the heir of nature, is poor. . . . . The World . . . . has reached a fertility which can give every human being a plenty undreamed of even in the Utopias. But between this plenty . . . . and the people hungering for it, step the "cornerers," the syndicates, trusts, combinations, with the cry of "overproduction." . . . . Holding back the riches of earth, sea, and sky from their fellows who famish and freeze in the dark . . . . they declare . . . . that there is too much light and warmth and food. . . . . The majority have never been able to buy enough of anything; [the] minority have too much of everything to sell. . . . .

The writings of George and Bellamy and Lloyd, however, were only surface evidences of the deep unrest which the new conditions of urban industrialism had produced. They revealed a solid discontent; they emphasized the tendency to look to government as an agent of social betterment which the Civil War had begun; they showed that Americans still accepted without doubts the idea that Christianity offered a sound basis for genuine democratic practice in society. But they did not indicate that a great revolt was about to take place in

127

the name of democracy. They were not even directly related to the Populist uprising of the late 1880's and early 1890's.

The Populist movement was a queer mixture of anger over hard times and the privileges going to the capitalist class, and a genuine belief in and desire for a purer American democracy. It expressed the resentments of the rural world against the growing power of the city and its interests; it carried the fears of the farmers of South and West that their political strength was failing and that the parties no longer represented their interests; it revealed a growing hatred of the wealth and power in the hands of the few which seemed to be making democracy in America into a sham.

A Nebraska editor wrote:

There are three great crops raised in Nebraska. One is a crop of corn, one a crop of freight rates, and one a crop of interest. One is produced by farmers who by sweat and toil farm the land. The other two are produced by men who sit in their offices and behind bank counters, and farm the farmers. The corn is less than half a crop. The freight rates will produce a full average. The interest crop, however, is the one that fully illustrates the boundless resources and prosperity of Nebraska. When corn fails the interest yield is largely increased.

James Baird Weaver of Iowa declared in 1892: "This is no longer a country governed by the people" but one of "Federal Monopolies." Judge David Davis of Illinois was filled "with apprehension" by "the rapid growth of corporate powers . . . . and their corrupting influence at the seat of government, their overshadowing influence among party managers from county primaries to National Conventions. . . . ." The *Western Rural* insisted:

The fact is becoming more and more apparent as the years go by that the lines are becoming distinctly drawn between the class who live by rewards of manual labor and an aristocracy which subsists upon the profits acquired from other people's earnings. Mammon is enthroned and reason debased in the dispensation of God's providence . . . . by which . . . . the natural wealth, which belongs to the many, [is] in the hands of the few. . . . .

In his volume, *A Call to Action*, Weaver pointed out the "ghastly condition of American society" and declared that unless

the people of America shall immediately take political matters into their own hands, the contrasts [between wealth and poverty] portend a tragic future. The millionaire and the pauper cannot, in this country, long dwell together in peace, and it is idle to attempt to patch up a truce between them. Enlightened self-respect and a quickened sense of justice are impelling the multitude to demand an interpretation of the anomalous spectacle . . . . presented before their eyes, of a world filled with plenty and yet multitudes of people suffering for all that goes to make life desirable. They are calling to know why idleness should dwell in luxury and those who toil in want; and they are inquiring why one-half of God's children should be deprived of homes upon a planet which is large enough for all.

And Weaver was a safe, sane, Iowa man, moved by a deep love of Jefferson's democracy. He had not been drinking at poisoned foreign fountains. He spoke because: "The aristocratic classes of the old country [were] constantly point[ing] their turbulent striving masses to the United States, in proof that republics afford no refuge or hope to the oppressed millions of mankind. . . . ."

The preamble to the Populist platform of 1892 declared:

We meet in the midst of a Nation brought to the verge of moral, political, and material ruin. Corruption dominates the ballot box, the legislatures, the Congress, and touches even the ermine of the bench. The people are demoralized. . . . . The newspapers are largely subsidized or muzzled, public opinion silenced, business prostrated, our homes covered with mortgages, labor impoverished, and the land concentrating in the hands of the capitalists. From the same prolific womb of governmental injustice we breed two classes—tramps and millionaires.

William Allen White, bitter enemy of the Populists, sensed the deep union of democracy and Christianity behind the movement when he described it as "a fanaticism like the Crusades." He writes:

Indeed, the delusion that was working on the people took the form of religious frenzy. Sacred hymns were torn from their pious tunes to give place to words that deified the cause [of silver] and made gold—and all its symbols, capital, wealth, plutocracy—diabolical. At night, from ten thousand little white schoolhouse windows, lights twinkled back vain hope to the stars. . . . . Far into the night the voices rose—women's voices, children's voices, the voices of old men, of youths and of maidens, rose on the ebbing prairie breezes, as the crusaders of the revolution rode home, praising the people's will as though it were God's will and cursing wealth for its iniquity.

We can follow developments only to notice that the whole great impulse at length found its spokesman and leader in the person of William Jennings Bryan, of Illinois and Nebraska, who always preferred to be called "The Christian Statesman." Minus a golden voice Bryan would have been a typical midwesterner. He was "average" and he was thoroughly Amer-

131

ican. The men of the Mississippi Valley always understood him and respected him, even if they did not vote for him. More people shook his hand and said "God bless you" than to any other American of his day. The people of the West never understood why eastern men called him clownish and classed him with Phineas Barnum and Brigham Young.

His forebears were typical pioneers of upland-southern stock. They followed well-beaten trails into Illinois and repeated the experiences of thousands of their kind who sought a home and new opportunity in the new West. Of his ancestors, Bryan once wrote: "There is not among them so far as I know, one of great wealth or great political or social prominence, but so far as I have been able to learn they were honest, industrious, Christian, moral, religious people—not a black sheep in the flock, not a drunkard, not one for whose life I would have to apologize." That was all any mid-westerner could ask of ancestors. He, himself, was born at Salem, Illinois, in 1860, and grew to manhood on a diet of Sunday schools and pious platitudes. His father was a Baptist, his mother a Methodist; he attended both Sunday schools each Sunday and in the end became a Presbyterian. His favorite songs were hymns— "One Sweetly Solemn Thought" and "I'll Go Where You Want Me To Go, Dear Lord." He was tolerant of all religious beliefs; he was bitterly intolerant of all unbelief. He was confident that the American people would never elect William Howard Taft to the presidency because Taft was a Unitarian.

Bryan graduated at a small western denominational college with a reputation for oratory which broke out on such subjects as "Character," "Justice," and "Individual Powers." He studied law in Chicago under Lyman Trumbull, Lincoln's old friend, and then moved to Nebraska and entered politics. Without pull or favors he won his way against odds and in less than two years turned a normal seven thousand Republican majority into a three thousand Democratic majority. He took his seat in Congress to oppose the tariff and to fight privilege in the interest of the common man. Jefferson was his hero and his model.

In his thinking Bryan was typically western and rural. He believed that the farmers were the real producers and that the cities and industry depended on the farmer for their prosperity. He knew that farming did not produce great quantities of money for its people. Few could ever rise above the level of what was described as being "well fixed." Most farmers would have to depend on the increasing value of their acres, the unearned increment, for any considerable amount of wealth. That magnified their desire to own land, led them into debt, and gave them the debtors' outlook. But it made them anything but communists and social radicals. It aroused their distrust of those who piled up great wealth in manufacturing, banking, railroading, or some other nonagricultural way. Bryan was wont to say that few men could earn a million dollars, and if they did, they would be too busy earning it to collect it. He implied that those who had collected a million dollars had spent their time collecting, not earning, the money. Yet honest toil and an honest return from toil and even from foresight, as in the purchase of real estate, were good. A modest fortune evidenced service rendered; the failure of hard-working farmers to prosper indicated the failure of democracy itself.

In the middle of the 1890's, when corporations and trusts waxed fat and the western farmers suffered from droughts, debts, mortgages, and high freight rates, William Jennings Bryan, commoner, fused the economic discontent, the Populist gospel, and the old Jeffersonian ideals into a new western revolt. His deep sincerity and his powerful oratory enabled him to crowd aside the old leadership of the Democratic party and to become in 1896 its candidate for the presidency of the United States. But Bryan was leading both more and less than the Democratic party. He was the head of the whole bitter revolt of lesser men against the new urban-industrial America and its values. It was a mere accident that he marched under the banners of that party. He was speaking a truth far more significant than he knew when he once remarked: "When I attempt to preach a sermon they accuse me of delivering a Democratic speech; and when I deliver a Democratic speech they accuse me of preaching a sermon."

The whole sum and substance of Bryan's appeal lay in his perfect fusing of the democratic ideals, the Christian principles, and the farmers' bitterness at both loss of prestige and failure to prosper. He expressed it all in his first great speech at the Chicago Convention. "I come to speak to you" he said, "in defense of a cause as holy as the cause of liberty—the cause of humanity." It was not a question of persons; it was a question of principle. He accused the eastern businessmen of disturbing the business interest of the West and of making the definition of "a businessman" too limited in its application. The term should include all those who toiled—the worker as well as his employer, the country lawyer and the cross-roads merchant as well as those who directed industry and banking in the great cities. What America needed was "an Andrew Jackson to stand, as Jackson stood, against the encroachments of organized wealth." He would stand with Thomas Jefferson on the money question and insist that "the issue of money is a function of government, and that the banks ought to go out of the governing business. . . . ." "There are two ideas of government," he said. "There are those who believe that if you will only legislate to make the well-to-do prosperous, their prosperity will leak through on those below. The Democratic idea, however, has been that if you make the masses prosperous, their prosperity will find its way up through every class which rests upon them."

You come to us and tell us that the great cities are in favor of the gold standard; we reply that the great cities rest upon our broad and fertile prairies. Burn down your cities and leave our farms, and your cities will spring up again as if by magic; but destroy our farms and the grass will grow in the streets of every city in the country. . . . . Having behind us the producing masses of this nation and the world, supported by the commercial interests, the laboring interests and the toilers everywhere, we will answer their demand for a gold standard by saying to them: You shall not press down upon the brow of labor this crown of thorns, you shall not crucify mankind upon a cross of gold.

This speech has been called an oratorical triumph. It probably was that, but it was much more. Through William Jennings Bryan the whole great rural world had become articulate. He had voiced the protest of the old America against the overshadowing dominance of a new urban-industrial order. He had talked as farmers wanted to talk; he had talked like hard-handed men who daily read their Bibles, said their family prayers, and listened on the quiet Sabbath to the Protestant ministers' sermons. He had revealed their distrust of the new ways to wealth and the greater wealth they yielded;

their hatred of privilege and corruption in politics for private gain; their contempt for the
new aristocracy which revealed itself in city
ways; their feeling that honest toil should give
prosperity. He had called America back to old
principles and doctrines—principles and doctrines as old as Jackson and Jefferson. He had
launched another democratic revolt just as Lincoln had done in 1860. The money issue was
merely a tragic symbol. The real issue was the
old America. One day Bryan would climax his
lifework in a great battle against evolution,
against science—the handmaid of industry and
the modern age! That was as it should have
been.

Eastern interests understood this better than
Bryan himself. The *New York Herald* called his
speech "a shot as dangerous and treasonable as
that fired on Sumter in '61 . . . ." and referred
to his followers as "the Jacobins of the West
and South." It accused Bryan of "mouthing
resounding rottenness," and charged him with
being "a puppet in the blood-imbued hands of
Altgeld, the anarchist, Debs, the revolutionist,
and other desperadoes of that stripe." "None
of his masters," however, it quickly added,

"were more apt than he at lies and forgeries
and blasphemies and all the nameless iniquities
of that campaign against the Ten Command-
ments." The Reverend Cortland Myers, of the
Baptist Temple, declared with pious intemperance that the chief issue of this campaign "directly affected the gospel of Calvary" and announced that he would devote his sermons from
that time until election day to denouncing the
Chicago platform. He was doing battle against
a revolution and nothing less than a revolution.

In the tangling of basic democratic revolt
with the money question lies the tragedy of the
campaign of 1896. Bryan, as a rule, felt correct-
ly on fundamental issues; he could not, however, always think straight about them. The
economic depression which gripped his farmers
and his West was too immediate and too pressing, and the temptation to concentrate on hard
times and the remedy for them too great for his
capacities. He made silver the symbol of democracy, and at the same time the remedy for
the ills of the day. Gold, too, became a symbol and the fight was reduced to one between
the metals and not one between democrats and
aristocrats of the new kind. Mark Hanna's

clever campaign of education, centering about an imaginary full dinner-pail, shifted the issue completely. The fate of the old democratic America was linked with the soundness or unsoundness of "16-to-1." The question of equality and security for the masses in a new urban-industrial America was never faced.

This democratic uprising was like that led by Jefferson, that by Jackson, and that by Lincoln in most of its essentials. It differed from them primarily in the fact that they had triumphed; this one failed and failed hopelessly. Thus was revealed the fact that basic changes had taken place in America and that the democratic problem was different. Those who looked beneath the surface noted that the old isolation which had marked our national life since the Monroe Doctrine was first proclaimed was rapidly passing. Two years after Bryan's defeat we were to fight a war with Spain and add a far-flung empire to our possessions. The Atlantic and the Pacific narrowed. In 1890 the census declared that the frontier was at an end. It could find no region within our borders which could be so designated. That, said Professor Turner, "marked the closing of a great historical movement." Shortly after 1900 the president of the United States began calling meetings of state governors and other interested parties for the purpose of considering the sad state of our national resources. They were badly depleted. Most of them had long since passed into private hands. A movement to conserve these resources for the future was imperative.

About the same time others began to see that the American farmer had made most of his profits in the past from the steady increase in the value of his lands, from the spending of the natural fertility of his soils, and from the low level at which he lived on the farm awaiting the time when he could retire to the country town or move to California. They began to suggest that these three sources of profit were about ended. Lands would rise, but not in such a steady way as to give each generation a retirement fund. Soils were being depleted and fertilizers must soon be returned to the lands and their tending become scientific, hence more expensive. Urban standards of living were slowly creeping into the country and the way of life had to be even more drastically altered if the young people were to be persuaded to remain on the farms. In other words, the great natural forces which had worked in America for freedom and equality and given the peculiar quality to our life which we proudly called "the American way" or "the democratic way" were beginning to pass or had already passed. The future belonged to the city, to industry, to a new kind of agriculture. America was turning around again to face Europe. American democracy in the future would have to test itself against other systems and prove its effectiveness as a national force.

The Bryan revolt, therefore, marked the end of an era in the history of American democracy. Up until that time great natural forces in our economic and social life, over which we exercised no control, had dictated a democratic life for us based largely on a high average standard of living. Because of the great natural resources and the American way of occupying the continent, we needed only to emphasize freedom. Equality had taken care of itself most of the time and had been able, when occasion required, to win through revolt. Isolation, the frontier, the farm, and free land required only freedom to give a high degree of equality and thus round out the democratic dogma. Well might government keep its hands off; well might we boast of "the land of the free." But freedom under urban industrialism had proved to be something else. It had too often meant freedom to exploit and to lift the few above the many. It had produced America's first real aristocracy. Slums and share-croppers and class hatred had become a normal part of national life.

If democracy was to live, the emphasis had to shift from freedom to the other ingredient of the dogma, equality. If men were to be equal, however, they could no longer achieve equality for themselves. Government would have to become more active. Democracy would be a choice from then on. It would have to be planned if it were to continue to exist. And all this in the face of strong men, also born out of the American experience, who had no interest or desire for either freedom or equality for anyone except themselves. Somehow or other a balance would have to be made. That was the new problem facing a people who had never even taken the trouble to define democracy or to inquire into its meaning either as a theory or as a practice in American life.

INDEX

INDEX

Gardening, 75, 80

George, Henry, 125–26, 127

Gettysburg, 68

Giddings, Joshua, 98

Gold standard, 137, 139

Government: an agent of social betterment, 127; checks and balances of, 5, 34; consolidation of, 16, 72, 97; and the Constitution, 26; by the few, 13, 143; by force, 22; by majorities, 51; local, 9, 17, 97; of the people, by the people, for the people, 68, 101; purposes of, 32–35; restriction of, 23–27, 34–35; right of people to alter, 26–27; tyranny of, 22, 34; western ideas of, 59

Great Lakes, 80, 83

Group patterns, conformity to, 47, 50

Hamilton, Alexander, 16

Hamiltonian theory of government, 13, 16, 17–18, 24

Hanna, Mark, 139–40

Happiness of the individual, 20–21, 26, 27, 31–34, 66, 126

Harrington, James, 4

Harvey, George B., 112

Hill, Edwin C., 112

Homestead legislation, 108, 110, 119, 120

Homesteads, 71, 97, 101

Hovey, Carl, 112

Immigration, 108

Improvements, interval, 54, 55, 61, 97

Independence, 5, 6, 12, 17

Individualism, 7–11, 27, 46, 47, 95

Industrial aristocracy, 77

Industrial Revolution, 40, 73–75, 81, 107

Industrialism, urban, 127

Industries of New England, shift in, 74–77

Internal improvements; *see* Improvements, internal

Iron, 108

Iron manufacturing, 81

Isolation, 142; American, passing of, 140

Izard, Ralph, 44

Jackson, Andrew, 43, 52, 55, 59, 82, 136, 138, 140; appeal to common people, 57–58; election of, 56, grievances leading to, 57–58; inaugural, 58–59; "reign" of, 59; symbol of the new West, 60; war against national bank, 62–64

Jefferson, Thomas, 12, 14, 19–20, 52, 54, 59, 103, 125, 126, 136, 138, 140; defense of democracy, 17–18; presidency of, 35–37

Jeffersonian democracy, basic principles of, 20–35

Justice, 43, 73

"Kingdom of Cotton," 82–83

Labor, 39; child, 67, 77–79; contempt for, 112–13; foreign, 67, 71, 75, 110–11; native, 67, 75; organization of, 116–18; working conditions of, 75, 77–79

Labor union formed by mechanics of Philadelphia, 90

Labor unions, 117–18; opposition to, 118

Lands, 8, 53, 55; free, 3–4, 41, 54, 66, 142; public, 61, struggle for easier access to, 64–65

Law, transitory nature of, 28

Lee, Henry, 77

Leisure, 105, 114

Levelers, the, 4

INDEX